Praise for *The Untrue Story of You*:

'The Untrue Story of You *offers one of the most significant advances in our understanding of who we are, why we do what we do and what we can do to end the negative patterns that hold us back. This beautiful and inspiring book has all the hallmarks of a spiritual classic.'*
JOHN GRAY, AUTHOR OF INTERNATIONAL BESTSELLER MEN ARE FROM MARS, WOMEN ARE FROM VENUS

'This book has so many layers that it will resonate for weeks after you've finished the final page. It is the story of forgiveness of an abusive past, a visionary work of original philosophy, an original theory of what it means to be human in all its complexity and a practical toolkit for overcoming the demons of your past. This is one book you will be buying in bulk and thrusting into the hands of every one of your friends.'*
MARCI SHIMOFF, NEW YORK TIMES BESTSELLING AUTHOR OF HAPPY FOR NO REASON, CHICKEN SOUP FOR THE WOMAN'S SOUL AND FEATURED TEACHER IN THE MOVIE THE SECRET

'Heal the story of pain and set yourself free! Bryan Hubbard presents a unique work that is carefully researched, sensitively written, hugely insightful and, above all, helpful!'*
ROBERT HOLDEN, AUTHOR OF SHIFT HAPPENS!

'I believe you have come up with a truly valuable model for personal growth. It is both straightforward and easily graspable on the one hand and potentially powerful and downright transformational on the other. The world would be well served by your using this innovative approach to touch many, many people globally.'*
BILL BAUMAN, AUTHOR OF THE ULTIMATE HUMAN

'This is a book of big ideas about who you are but also big solutions about what's holding you back. The deceptively simple theory of this book stays with you for weeks after you have finished the final page, but also arms you with the tools to reclaim your life. It picks up where* The Power of Now *leaves off.*
JANET ATTWOOD, AUTHOR OF THE INTERNATIONAL BESTSELLER THE PASSION TEST

What readers are saying:

'It's an amazing read. I picked it up and read it in a day. Why? Well, I just couldn't put it down. The concept is so simple and yet so powerful. In fact, I've mentioned it to all my friends and family. A must-read!'
DEBRA QUARLES

'It is wonderful how even internal questions are always answered, and in the most amazing ways at times... it's like breadcrumbs leading us on the way home.'
REGINA JAGNE

'The first time I read the book I literally danced all the way around our house. It was mad, but through your words for the first time "I got it". I really got the idea of being free and light and the idea of being a free spirit inside this human body was within my grasp!'
SARA MYNARD

'This is the most wonderful book I have ever read. A gift to humanity.'
SHAUN PETERSEN

'This book is what I've been waiting for – it's just the best book, and it made spirituality so simple.'
ARDRE BURGOYNE

THE ~~TRUE~~ Untrue STORY OF YOU

THE ~~TRUE~~ Untrue STORY OF YOU

How to Let Go of the Past that Creates You,
and Become Fully Alive in the Present

BRYAN HUBBARD

HAY HOUSE

Carlsbad, California • New York City • London • Sydney
Johannesburg • Vancouver • Hong Kong • New Delhi

First published and distributed in the United Kingdom by:
Hay House UK Ltd, Astley House, 33 Notting Hill Gate, London W11 3JQ
Tel: +44 (0)20 3675 2450; Fax: +44 (0)20 3675 2451; www.hayhouse.co.uk

Published and distributed in the United States of America by:
Hay House Inc., PO Box 5100, Carlsbad, CA 92018-5100
Tel: (1) 760 431 7695 or (800) 654 5126; Fax: (1) 760 431 6948 or (800) 650 5115
www.hayhouse.com

Published and distributed in Australia by:
Hay House Australia Ltd, 18/36 Ralph St, Alexandria NSW 2015
Tel: (61) 2 9669 4299; Fax: (61) 2 9669 4144; www.hayhouse.com.au

Published and distributed in the Republic of South Africa by:
Hay House SA (Pty) Ltd, PO Box 990, Witkoppen 2068
Tel/Fax: (27) 11 467 8904; www.hayhouse.co.za

Published and distributed in India by:
Hay House Publishers India, Muskaan Complex, Plot No.3, B-2,
Vasant Kunj, New Delhi 110 070; Tel: (91) 11 4176 1620; Fax: (91) 11 4176 1630
www.hayhouse.co.in

Distributed in Canada by:
Raincoast Books, 2440 Viking Way, Richmond, B.C. V6V 1N2
Tel: (1) 604 448 7100; Fax: (1) 604 270 7161; www.raincoast.com

A significant portion of this book was originally published as
Time-Light (New Age Publishing, 2011).

Text © Bryan Hubbard, 2014

The moral rights of the author have been asserted.

The information given in this book should not be treated as a substitute for
professional medical advice; always consult a medical practitioner. Any use of
information in this book is at the reader's discretion and risk. Neither the author
nor the publisher can be held responsible for any loss, claim or damage arising out
of the use, or misuse, of the suggestions made, the failure to take medical advice or
for any material on third party websites.

A catalogue record for this book is available from the British Library.

ISBN: 978-1-78180-466-7

Contents

Part III: The 21-Day Time-Light Programme

> *'Verily I say unto you, Except ye be converted, and become as little children, ye shall not enter into the kingdom of heaven.'*
> MATTHEW, 18.3

> *'Hell is other people.'*
> JEAN-PAUL SARTRE

> *'Hell is thinking there are other people.'*
> BRYAN HUBBARD

For Lynne, who lights up my time

Foreword

The first thing I noticed about Bryan was his laugh. I was a fellow editor in the shabby offices of a British publishing company in 1985 and, newly separated at the time from a three-year-old marriage, had very little to smile about.

We'd been in the middle of an otherwise uneventful corporate meeting of the company's editorial and advertising staff when the proceedings were interrupted by an outburst from one corner of the room. An entire editorial team was convulsed in giggles, led by the editor, the loudest of the group.

This was no ordinary laugh – this deep baritone burst open the silence, seeped into every corner, and rained down on every person seated in the room. Indeed, as I discovered when I heard it again in subsequent weeks, Bryan's laugh was fully capable of traversing walls. Although it soon had everyone in the room laughing along – a particularly dour group ordinarily – these were not simply copycat gestures. They represented the shock of recognition that occurs when the listener is a rare witness to joy emerging straight from within soul.

The resonance of that laugh was all the more astonishing to me after I got to know Bryan in the months that followed and learned something of his history. As a child Bryan had been a victim of abuse – not physical abuse but mental cruelty of the most potentially debilitating kind. His father, George, an intelligent, if emotionally arrested man, had been severely disappointed in his own life and consequently vented most of his frustration with its shortcomings on his young son – usually in the form of a venomous sarcasm.

Bryan had been his father's unwanted third child from a second marriage – and a constant reminder of his own failure to create a loving relationship, particularly with his first wife, who preferred to have her two children taken away from her rather than live with George for one more day.

George refused to acknowledge his son by name and never missed an opportunity to belittle, shout at, or in some way verbally abuse him. Although Bryan was extremely intelligent, his father placed him in a school for tough delinquents, where he essentially survived only by nimble verbal sleight of hand.

George wasn't content to ignore his youngest son's prodigious gifts but did his best to crush them, ignoring a letter from Bryan's school recommending that he apply to Oxford University, so that he was made to leave school at 16. Bryan's mother Edie adored him, but as an orphan who'd never had any parental figures in her own life, and as George's other target, she'd had no blueprint for how to become an encouraging parent.

In a sense, Bryan had to grow up and launch his subsequent career as a successful journalist, publisher and entrepreneur in spite of his parents. Often in such a desolate landscape, humour becomes a sanctuary, as does deep spiritual inquiry. Bryan became a spiritual seeker during his early teenage years, and it was no accident that when he put himself through university as an adult, he pursued a degree in philosophy.

From my perspective, this backstory didn't accord in any way with the happy, sensitive person in front of me and the exemplary father he became to our two daughters – except at certain moments. During the course of our joyful 30-year partnership I've observed as Bryan's past occasionally hovers over him like an unwelcome phantom.

In response to some stimulus – a slightly raised voice or the mildest of challenges – he'd angrily lash out. I was stunned by this outsize response until I realized what was going on. He wasn't having a conversation with me. He was still talking to George. He was, as he would now put it, time-heavy, trying to put to rest something unresolved from his past.

Over time, I observed this phantom making an appearance with less and less frequency. Bryan preferred mapping the journey to his own understanding and healing rather than taking the ride with a therapist, and like most creative people, he sought to universalize his experience so that ultimately he could help others as well as himself. As he observed the process of shedding his own phantoms, he began to consider the possibility that the past exists as a separate self in all of us – and becomes, in most cases, the bully of the other selves.

One day, when I returned from a trip, his theory of the Three Selves emerged, fully formed, as if pulled out of thin air, and Bryan then spent many months refining it. Although there are certain parallels with other disciplines, I've yet to find another model that answers so much about the complexity of the human experience with such profound simplicity.

Other theories that attempt to define consciousness fall short because they don't encompass the intricacies of our lives and the full range of human potential. The majority of programmes promising enlightenment fail precisely because they don't take into account the subversive power of the past.

Besides examining the largely negative effect of the past self and how it becomes like a permanent unwanted guest, the Three Selves model also provides a brilliant answer to so many of the big questions man has never had adequate answers for – from events that take place 'outside of time', such as remote viewing or near-death experiences, to human consciousness and its 'life' outside of the physical body. As such, the theory resonates perfectly with my own work on *The Field*, *The Bond* and the power of consciousness.

In addition to laying out one of the most plausible theories I've ever read about what it means to be human, this book arms the reader with a powerful set of tools. The step-by-step programme is a comprehensive guide to shedding the burdens of the past and becoming time-light – and so free, as Bryan puts it, 'to fall back in love with your life'.

This resonates so deeply because it speaks with the authentic truth of personal experience. Ultimately, this book represents Bryan's journey, from the pain and darkness of unexamined adversity to understanding and recovered wholeness. May you take to the road with him and learn to travel light.

Lynne McTaggart
London, July 2014

Introduction

There's a radical, and transformative, idea at the heart of this book:

The thought thinks the thinker.

This feels uncomfortable, not right, and certainly counterintuitive. We're so used to the concept that 'I' think, and, indeed, control my thoughts, that it's impossible to conceive that this mighty 'I' is actually a fiction and creation of thought itself.

For me to demonstrate that this heretical idea is true, I also need to explain what thought is and how it arises. This book will show how the sense of 'I' is created through experiences that are only partially understood; almost every experience is partially understood, by the way, because it's invariably seen only from your own perspective. And your many thoughts generate many 'Is' that often contradict each other.

The essential message is that most of mankind operates from a universal sense of mistaken identity – you aren't what you think you are. The 'I' that's thought into being masks your true self, which is the doorway to real and lasting happiness. Understanding ourselves in and through time is the key to this doorway, and to a life that's always in the present and joyful.

It's also the essence of most of the world's great religions – teaching us to understand the creation of a self through time is their ultimate aim, even if this isn't always explicitly stated. For example, Jesus's pivotal teachings concern man in time. He taught us to take 'no thought of the morrow', and his exhortation to 'become as little children' is his call for us to live in the present moment, without the weight of the past and its reach into an imagined future.

The Buddha said something similar; according to *The Dhammapada*, he declared, 'What we are today comes from our thoughts of yesterday, and our present thoughts build our life of tomorrow: our life is the creation of our mind.' In the verse that follows, he then states, 'He insulted me, he hurt me, he defeated me, he robbed me. Those who think such thoughts won't be free from hate.' This statement is an expression of the movement of time through thoughts that create our reality. We think our world into being.

The Hindu Upanishads tell us: 'According as a man acts and walks in the path of life, so he becomes. He that does good becomes good; he that does evil becomes evil. By pure actions he becomes pure; by evil actions he becomes evil.'

These texts are trying to demonstrate that the key is in understanding the self in and through time, and that this self is entirely a construct of thought. Strangely, the sense of self is the one thing that we never define. Instead, we assume we already know what we are because, after all, what could be closer than our thoughts?

And because we've become hypnotized into believing there's a permanent self that constantly thinks and analyzes, we turn to therapy in order to improve it – make it less angry or obsessive, perhaps – or to the guru in order to become enlightened. But what's there to improve or enlighten if the whole construct is nothing more substantial than a thought-form, so much smoke in the wind?

The great religions and the mystics have all tried different messages through the ages to help us unlock the door. We've been told variously to overcome the ego, to transcend ourselves, to be still. Even today, we're reminded of the power of 'now'.

The key to a transcendent life lies in an understanding of the self as both a process of time and outside of time: the power of *how*, if you will. This book, and the Time-Light programme at its heart, gives you the true meaning and reward of every religion. Ultimately, no religion, method or philosophy captures your depth and mystery. You'll even come to view the programme as a necessary step along the way, but one that you've grown beyond.

In its place will be you as a natural being, a 'time-light' person. Then you'll be able to bring into the world the full potential you were born to deliver. You'll understand that you're part of a unified field, and that you're connected to everything and everyone. Your fate won't be that of so many, who are inhabited by a past whose heaviness wore them down until life wasn't worth living.

The Untrue Story of You:
Essential Points

The golden rule:

That to which you don't fully attend will weigh you down.

- Each of us has our own story – a myth by which we live – which colours our world, and determines the life we lead.

- Your story is derived from your experiences, your family and forebears. It's more than a memory, though: it's an energy imprint. This energy is the catalyst for thoughts and emotions, which create a 'you' in the process. Although you live your life as though there's a continuous you in command, the reality is that *the thought thinks the thinker*.

- Your story isn't true. It's an impression from events that were seen almost entirely from your perspective alone, and without taking into account the circumstances, other people and their motivations.

- Because you're a construct of the past from experiences, you're a phenomenon of time: present, past and potential. As such, you have Three Selves, or time-bodies:

1. Your Present time-body, or self, includes your body, your brain and the world that you witness in time and space. It has a simple memory based upon bodily needs, protection, safety, and so on.

2. The Past time-body, or self, has three layers, depending on the type of experience: Knowledge (a remembrance of ability and learning), Narrative (your name, religion, nationality, and so on) and Psychological (memory of the events that form the major part of your story).

3. The Potential centre, or self, is outside of time and space. It's an impersonal self that's also known as universal or collective consciousness, but it finds expression in time and space through a body. In its passive state, the Potential is the silent witness to every experience, and is the only true source of a sense of a continuous self, while we're awake and sleep. But because it's impersonal, this sense of a self is not you!

- The past accumulates when we don't fully witness the experience in the moment. A fully witnessed experience leaves no energetic print.

- As the past builds, so too does a sense of space, which creates a feeling of separation and, ultimately, isolation from the world.

- Pulses from the past's energy imprinting are attempts by the Past time-body in particular to achieve completion and final understanding. Experience happens only in time and space, and the past seeks to relive experiences that we never completely understood in the first place. From this, patterns are created in our life.

- Addictions are also repeat patterns that seek final and complete understanding. They're not always from an impulse to forget, nor are they always born of sadness: they can also be energy waves that seek to remember, originating from moments of ecstasy and unity.

- We have neither a subconscious nor an unconscious; instead, we have energy centres that seek resolution. Far from being suppressed, all of our thoughts and feelings, even the most subliminal, are constantly pulsing to the Present time-body, which is the only centre in which they can be played out and resolved.

- The ultimate purpose of life is to understand and so dissolve the past, in order to give full expression to the Potential self in the world.

PART I

THE UNTRUE STORY
OF YOU AND TIME

Chapter 1
The Untrue Story of Me

'Time is the substance from which I am made.
Time is a river which carries me along, but I am
the river; it's a tiger that devours me, but I am the
tiger; it's a fire that consumes me, but I am the fire.'

Jorge Luis Borges

For years, I struggled with chronic depression. There was no apparent cause: I had a wonderful marriage, two daughters of whom I'm deeply proud, a great little publishing business, and a lovely home. Despite this material success, a grey fog enveloped me always. I saw little or no point in going on – life had no meaning or value, and I couldn't find joy in anything.

At one particularly low point, I almost broke down into tears after passing a bridal gown shop: I just felt so sorry for those hopeful young women, starting out on a new life with their husband, so optimistic and full of hopes, plans and dreams.

I also carried around a sense that I just wasn't good enough, and, of course, that became a self-fulfilling prophecy – not because I failed, but because I wouldn't even *try*. Yet, as I'd discover later, this was but one of my selves, or voices; a dominant one, perhaps, but not the only one.

We all have hundreds of selves prompted by different memories. Another voice could contradict the one that created a 'me' that was worthless, and instead tell me I was worthwhile. There was also a compensatory twist – I was conceited. This is a common, albeit paradoxical, phenomenon that can arise from a sense of being undeserving.

Who's depressed?

It was around that time that something in me finally said 'enough', and my relationship with my wife, Lynne, had a great deal to do with that moment of waking. It's a truism that we can see ourselves only in relationship to others, but when you have someone as challenging as Lynne, you really start to see yourself!

As a philosophy graduate, my way into the problem of depression was through the wide and perplexing portal of self-identity. Put it another way: who am I, or, what is this that's depressed? It's the perennial question that's kept philosophers busy for more than 2,000 years, and their answers seemed to ricochet between having a soul and just being a 'smart brain' in a body.

Modern neuroscience and biology lean towards the smart brain theory. Essentially, it argues that I'm nothing more or less than a collection of thoughts and memories, which will disappear forever on the death of the body. But this didn't feel quite right to me. Although part of my theory does indeed suggest something similar, it also points to something far richer about us that gets masked by the torrent of our thoughts.

After all, if I'm nothing more than a series of thoughts, *what* is suffering from depression? It reminds me of the joke of the old man speaking to a Zen master, and saying: 'If I don't exist, whose lumbago is this?'

To me, there was something missing in the smart brain theory, something that failed to capture the richness and complexity of our lives. How could I be nothing and yet still feel that I was somehow more than that? There always seems to be the observer, looking with utter disinterest at our thoughts and actions, and, when we sleep, at our dreams. So what *is* that?

To the smart brain theorist, my chronic depression could be explained away as a chemical imbalance, but, again, this minimized what had happened to me, and to the countless others similarly experiencing the condition. My depression – and I suspect that of my fellow sufferers – had an existential element to it. It was a shout against the life we lead – that somehow it should be better than this – and no pill was going to change that.

There were also the much bigger problems that trouble any thinking person: why is man always at war; how can we stand by and let so many children starve to death in a world that has plenty; what sort of a world are we creating for our children to inherit? Perhaps there were no answers to these big issues, but I sensed that if I could answer the 'what am I?' question, everything else might become a little clearer.

After all, I and the billions of others on Earth have created this world – its political systems, its trade laws and everything else that shapes it – and so defining the creator of the systems by which we live might also bring an understanding of the world and its problems.

That to which you don't fully attend

The 'who am I?' question puzzled me, picked at me, pinched me, pounded my head when I tried to sleep and pummelled me awake in the morning. The answer tumbled out of me in one session as I was sitting in the garden one afternoon. It started with my golden rule, such as it has become:

That to which you don't fully attend will weigh you down.

The sentence came fully formed, and it sounds rather biblical, but – thank goodness – nobody with a long white gown appeared to announce it. It seemed to have the gravitas of a commandment, perhaps the 11th tablet that was too much for Moses to carry down from the heights of Mount Sinai. But what did it mean?

At the prosaic level, it suggests we leave nothing undone when we carry out any transaction or relationship. The small print is initialled, all quarrels are resolved, and everyone leaves happy. But it has a much deeper meaning, too: if you're not fully in the moment, you'll have experiences that'll leave a mark – that mark is the past and it will weigh you down until you're time-heavy. You'll eventually become more the past than present.

When you say 'I', it could be any one of Three Selves speaking. These are based on different time sequences: the present, the past and potential. The present and past are creating energetic imprints, and these emit waves, or pulses, that are translated into thoughts and emotions and, in so doing, also create you.

That sudden rush of ideas was the result of every experience I'd had, every clue life had presented me, every person I'd met and every book I'd read. It happened to me there and then because everything that preceded that moment made it inevitable. I, as a point in space and time, was the perfect storm.

Let me immediately state that the way in which my answer to the 'who am I' question came gives it no special quality or authority. I offer it to you for you to test in your own life. Does it seem right to you? Does it resonate or have that ring of truth? Only you can decide. (Conversely, people of a sceptical disposition shouldn't dismiss the theory only because its origins were, for them, dubious. Again, look at it with an open mind and consider its merits.)

The two clues

For years afterwards, I challenged, attacked and argued against the theory, and worked it through and talked about it in workshops across the USA and the UK. When a therapist who attended one of the workshops told me that, after using the 'Three Selves' model he had achieved a remarkable breakthrough with one client whose problems had seemed intractable, I began to see there was something of value in the theory.

Yes, it happened in an instant, but my whole life had been a prelude to that moment. From all of this, two clues in particular stand out that helped me along my way.

The first happened with the death of my father. He was in his ninetieth year, and yet there was absolutely nothing wrong with him physically. A check-up a few years previously had revealed that he had the heart of someone 20 or 30 years younger. Yet, there he was, on the day I went to see him at his home, lying in bed.

'What's wrong?' I asked.

Nothing much, he replied with a shrug, other than that he'd had enough. He'd become tired of life, and now he wanted to die, he said. He turned away from me and faced the wall.

Hours later, as I was leaving, I put my head around the bedroom door and gave a tentative goodbye. I had a fleeting thought that it would be the last time I'd see him, even though the idea seemed absurd. He wished me well, and I left. Three days later my mother telephoned to tell me that my father had died.

In a sense, he'd wished his own death. There was no postmortem, but had there been one, the cause of death probably would have been something general and vague, and certainly not 'tired of life', or 'had enough', or even 'couldn't stand another day of this'.

If you're lucky, you'll die of old age. Doctors, family and friends will all agree that you had a good life. Medicine doesn't recognize old age as a cause of death, even though every day somebody seems to die from it. Certainly, your body gets 'worn out', or you lose the zest for life. You'll have seen much and, like my father, you'll have felt the enormous weight of past regrets, disappointments and hurts that you're carrying around. As the English poet William Wordsworth put it, 'The world is too much with us'.

On the day I visited my father, he was both a body that was talking to me in the bedroom in present time, and a past that seemed to inhabit him. In the end, that's what happens to most of us – the past bears down on us, as if it were a separate being, until we can't stand it, not even for one more day.

The other clue came to me years later, when I read a book about ghosts. Lynne was abroad, lecturing somewhere, my eldest daughter was at her university, and my youngest child was with friends. That left me with our pet dog, Ollie, and a shelf of books that I wanted to read. However, nothing I brought out into the garden seemed to hold my interest, so I wandered back into the house, and into Lynne's study, which is lined with books that she uses for her research.

I don't know why, but one book caught my attention. It was called *Visions of Immortality* (Element, 1998), by Ian Currie, a Canadian university professor who'd carried out a thorough review of the evidence for life after death, ghosts and apparitions. Perhaps it was the title, taken from a Wordsworth poem, or that it 'called me', as some books do to us, but whatever the reason, I took it from the shelf and back to my seat in the garden.

Until then, I'd had almost no interest in ghosts. I'd assumed they were either the creations of a fevered imagination or the inventions of attention-seekers. But I was astonished by what I read, and my preconceptions were turned on their head.

Currie had documented tale after tale of ghost stories or, more precisely, instances of contact with those who'd died. The stories were highly plausible, the people who related them had far more to lose than gain from the telling, and they were all independently verifiable. Currie demonstrated, beyond any reasonable doubt, that something of us survives death. But what is it?

It seemed to be something that still had unfinished business on Earth – invariably a message that had to be delivered through an emotionally charged entity. It wasn't physical – clearly not, as the body had died – and so it must be energetic. However, there's nothing extraordinary in that: physics tells us that everything, ultimately, is energy. Seen that way, it's reasonable to consider that our body and this 'ghost' that survives death are expressions of two different forms of energy.

Here was another demonstration that the past has an independent existence as a separate body of experiences, upsets, sadness, and trauma. It haunts us while we live, and eventually it kills us. According to Currie, it even lives on after we die. Whether or not you believe in ghosts, it's a potent metaphor for a past that seems to be another 'me' that lives in my body. The past is not just a collection of memories, but a palpable and energetic force that creates patterns in your life.

The genesis of my untrue story

So what of my untrue story – my myth that brought me to this point? What had happened that had cast such deep shadows that they darkened my adult life?

One of my earliest memories is of walking in the park with my mother and father. I must have been about three years old. I saw some litter on the ground. I picked it up, probably because it looked interesting rather than from any sense of good citizenry, and took it over to my father.

'That's right,' he said, 'now put it in the refuse receptacle.' I didn't know what a 'refuse receptacle' was any more than any three-year-old would, I suppose. So I stood there in front of him, still holding out the scrap of paper.

My father repeated his request, and I still stood there. He then screamed at me that I was stupid, that I would always be dumb. That was the last 'message' I got from my father for some four years. Until I was around seven years old, he just whistled for me as if I was the family dog.

My father was already well into his forties when I was born. His marriage to my mother had been his second, and, if truth be told, he married her primarily because he needed a carer for his two sons from his first marriage, which had ended in acrimonious divorce (and in an era when it was much more likely for the father to gain custody of the children). My birth, some six years after my father and mother married, was something that my mother truly wanted but which my father saw only as a necessary part of the marital contract: look after my two sons, and you can have a child yourself.

My father resented my arrival, and this was made clear by the way he treated me and spoke to me. It's no wonder that I grew up with a sense of being undeserving, that I would never amount to anything. I was reminded of it every day.

I hated my father. I lay awake in bed in the morning, waiting for him to leave the house and go to his work as an engineer at a nearby factory. As the door closed behind him, my world opened up and was bright. At night, before I could sleep I'd put imaginary guards around my bed.

Edie, my mother, was my ally and friend. But she was weak against the tyrant. Years later I discovered she'd gone 'into service' – working as a maid in a big house – when she was barely 16. So she didn't have too much self-confidence, and certainly not enough to stand up to the family bully.

I discovered there was another world: the 'inner' world of imagination where fountains of warm gold flowed all the time. I became an avid reader. I didn't *learn* how to read: at the age of four, I picked up a copy of *Alice in Wonderland* and just read it. That particular skill was quickly knocked out of me at school as teachers reminded me that what I did wasn't possible. After that I forgot how to read. So that was something else I discovered about my inner world. It could be limited by thoughts, and the beliefs of others.

I also had out-of-body experiences up until the age of 11. Every night I left my body and floated out of the window. It was a frightening experience, and I never welcomed it. I think out-of-body experiences are fairly common in children who are frightened or feel oppressed.

Why did my father behave the way he did? He burned with all the petty injustices he'd suffered over the years. The family was regaled at least once a week with tales of how, as a small boy, he'd had to walk to school in the snow one day, how he'd been wrongly accused of stealing an apple, how his sister was always the favourite... As he told us these stories about 'poor, poor George', as his mother used to describe him, his eyes would fill with tears and his face redden.

He was a very stingy man. In my first 16 years, I had only one summer holiday, I was never allowed to have a bike, and we all had to wash in a condemned sink in the kitchen because it cost too much to heat water in the boiler for a bath.

This meanness got to George's first wife. She went out dancing, got pregnant with another man, and left George and my two half-brothers. In those days settlements were determined by morality, and because George's wife was 'in the wrong' she was the unfit parent, and so her husband won full custody of the two boys.

Not that he wanted them; he immediately left them with his own mother while he went out drinking every night. But that couldn't last. He met my mother at a factory where they were both working as part of the war effort. Soon after the war they married and I was born in 1953.

The divorce burned deeper than anything else that had happened to George. It was pretty clear to me that he truly loved his first wife. He admitted he was prepared to take her back, even though she was carrying another man's child. But she couldn't stand being with him even one more day. From that, George cradled a lifelong hatred of women; he was always saying nasty things about them in general, and to my mother in particular.

My eldest half-brother, Terry, left the family home a year after I was born, and went as far away as he could – to New Zealand. He was around 21 at the time. He was a very intelligent boy but was never encouraged to go to university. Instead, he began an apprenticeship at a local engineering firm. My father was too cheap to buy Terry the proper overalls that all the other apprentices wore, and so instead he made do with pages from old newspapers that he wrapped around his arms and legs. He was a laughing stock.

When Terry left for New Zealand, my father promised to send on his precious record collection – he especially loved Brahms and Delius – but he never did. I discovered the records one evening when my parents were out; I suppose I was 12 or so. I played Brahms' First Symphony, and I was transfixed. I knew every note. Terry must have played it to me when I was a baby, and I still remembered it.

Years later, George discovered the records himself, while he was going through the attic with my other half-brother, Christopher. 'I promised to send these to Terry, and I never did.

I wasn't a good father,' he said, and Christopher thought he detected a tear in his father's eyes.

What's my name?

When I was around seven, my mother finally stood up to my father and demanded he call me by my name and talk to me properly instead of just whistling for me. He reluctantly agreed, although what he had to say was hardly life-affirming. I was regularly reminded of my stupidity, and how I would never amount to anything.

Monday nights were especially bad, as he'd come back from the Conservative Club, slightly intoxicated and very aggressive. George's aggression was never physical; instead, it was the exquisite put-down, expertly applied as though by a surgeon with a scalpel.

School was a welcome respite from the gloom at home. I was never a great scholar, but I never had any encouragement to be one. I took naturally to writing and drama: I was constantly chosen for the lead roles and I was even selected to give an oration at the local church in front of the town's great and good. Quite an honour.

My parents didn't turn up, but then they never came to any of my performances. I think my mother wanted to attend, but my father put a stop to it. The same thing happened to my year-end reports: although they were always good, my father barely read them. I remember bringing home one at an important stage of my development, when I was 16, and the English master saying in it that only one boy should go to Oxford, and that was me. I don't think my father could even be bothered to open the envelope.

My school was pretty rough – some of the boys from the bottom classes ended up in prison – but I enjoyed my time there, and it taught me how to take care of myself, usually by making the other boys laugh. I also brought the school great credit when I won a national writing award. The headmaster was astonished – in the 20 years he'd served at the school no boy had ever won an academic award.

My teacher's exhortations that I should go to Oxford, and my winning a national writing award, meant nothing to my father. There would be no further education for me; it was out to work at the age of 16, as it had been with my two half-brothers before me. I wanted to be a journalist, an ambition which elicited a snort from my father and a very raised eyebrow from the careers advisor at the school, whose advice was limited to two possibilities: local government for the brighter boys and engineering for the duller ones.

I was working in the town's hardware store when the local newspaper advertised for a new junior reporter, who would receive full training and minimal salary. Candidates needed to be 18 (I was 16), and have 'A' levels (I hadn't stayed at school to do them). Undaunted by my lack of qualifications, I applied.

To my surprise, I was granted an interview with the editor. He was a devout Christian who was a lay preacher at a nearby village church. He told me that more than 250 young people had applied for the role, and all were at least 18 and sufficiently qualified. My chances were slim to zero, he inferred, but he invited me to write an essay nonetheless.

My essay was chosen as the best and I was offered the job. My father thought luck or bribery had played a hand.

My inner world of imagination was getting stronger, and was more vivid and real to me than the world 'out there'. Having recently feasted on the French pessimists like Celine, I started to turn to philosophy, which felt immediately like home to me. I was drawn to the German metaphysicists, such as Schopenhauer and Nietzsche, as so many young men are, although the work of Kant looked unapproachable and unscalable. I climbed that intellectual mountain only as a mature philosophy student at London University.

I was also naturally drawn to mysticism. I met Jiddhu Krishnamurti and Andrew Cohen, and was among those who knew Barry Long, an Australian 'spiritual master', as he described himself, who later influenced Eckhart Tolle.

The patterns begin

Eventually I married, and the patterns of the past continued in my life. For a start, Angela, my wife, shared the same birthday as my mother, although what was to follow was beyond coincidence and was perplexing and mysterious.

I'd often wondered why my father was as nasty as he was, and why so much of it was aimed at me. Years later, I discovered why. I'm still not sure what inspired this, or how it came up in conversation, but one evening my parents revealed an intimate secret at the heart of their marriage. Astonishingly, the exact same problem lay at the heart of my marriage! Needless to say, my wife and I divorced soon after.

Patterns, patterns.

I saw that I had to get out and grab something of life, even though my self-esteem was almost non-existent. While I was editing a national magazine, I met Lynne, and the process of waking to my patterns began. She pointed out my self-imposed limitations and beliefs, which included an absurd inability to buy clothes for myself, as I didn't believe I deserved 'treats'. I was certainly conscious enough to know that I could never be as bad a father to my children as mine had been.

I would also lash out against any perceived insult or criticism, and my response was always Earth-scorching, flattening anything and anyone around me. It was always wildly disproportionate, and was distressing for the poor unfortunate on the receiving end of the barrage. Lynne's understanding of this process – that it was almost as though my father was inhabiting my body – was an important factor that kept our marriage together.

Any lesser person would probably have walked away. It was only when we adopted our second child that my mother revealed a secret that had caused her embarrassment and shame all her life: she'd been brought up in an orphanage. Seeing her son adopt a child helped her see it was no great shame after all.

Patterns, patterns.

I became far closer to my father towards the end of his life. His bitterness and resentment was replaced by a genuine interest, and even a level of respect for me and Lynne, and the work we were doing. On his deathbed, he called for me.

Reconciliation, forgiveness, understanding — these potent forces brought a symmetry and arc to a very troubled family dynamic, which is played out to different fugues and variations in most families.

Hating didn't change the old patterns, nor did an intellectual understanding – I'd tried both of those. For the transformation to happen, I had to completely understand *why* my father did what he did, understand his own suffering, and realize that nobody is born a monster, but only becomes so. I had to feel his hurts and the reasons why he did what he did. Forgiveness means a 360-degree view of the circumstances.

In that moment, I saw the situation in its totality – my parents, the circumstances, and me; in that moment, I finally experienced what had really happened. I saw my father as he truly was – a hurt child who'd never been appreciated or loved. I'd become part of his pattern, a victim of the energy flashes from his own past hurts. In that forgiveness, I was able to let my father go, and I became healthy and whole.

Much of this reconciliation happened before his death, but the understanding of the whole process became clear only when I had my 'Three Selves' revelation. Only then did I understand that the past not only haunts us, but *is* us. When we say 'I', it's rarely a reference to our body but instead points to a bundle of energetic pulses from the past.

It's imperative for us to understand the process of the past. As the Spanish philosopher George Santayana possibly said, 'Those who don't learn from history are doomed to repeat it', but more probably said, 'Those who can't remember the past are condemned to repeat it'. That's the ultimate struggle; the complete understanding of our past so that it dissolves, leaving that which is present to come forth.

Was I the change agent? No, because there is no 'I'! Instead of the patterns and processes, my past ceased to have a hold and lost its power to influence the present moment. This shift in energy or consciousness impacted everyone involved in the drama.

I regard my upbringing as fairly typical, and I know that many have suffered a far worse childhood than mine. Because of this, I've never spared even one moment's pity for myself. I tell my story only because people will wonder how I came to develop my theory of our Three Selves, and I wanted to use it as an illustration of how patterns are created in families and across the generations.

It also works as an example of how we create a story by which we live. My story, like every story, is untrue. It's untrue because we invariably have experiences that are exclusively from our perspective – by which I mean self-as-body perspective.

What I've come to understand is that my parents were doing the very best they could; that understanding on its own, if deeply felt and absorbed, is a releasing thought. I've come to have nothing but compassion and a deep love and gratitude for my parents. I understand now that the pain and grief we all endure is enough to make an angel weep.

The circle was completed a few years after my 'Three Selves' idea had started to form. Our older daughter, Caitlin, had left for university and we went with her to bring all the paraphernalia she needed for something that would form a shadow-play of a domesticated life. When we returned home, we found the most heartfelt letter from her, saying what extraordinary parents we'd been, and how she'd received the best possible start.

Patterns, patterns… starting to dissolve.

The Three Selves theory comes from witnessing pain and suffering. It's related to time, and how we're created through experience in space and time. The constant movement of the past masks the true beauty of us, which is timeless.

So let's begin *your* untrue story, and how it was created in time.

Chapter 2
The Untrue Story of You

'We are never living, but only hoping to live;
and looking forward always to being happy,
it's inevitable that we never are so.'

BLAISE PASCAL

We all have our story. We live by it, and it shapes us and the world we live in. If you were abused as a child, abuse may well become the primary colour of your life, and you may seek out more abuse because that's an endorsement of your story.

Your story can also colour the world in less vivid hues, but it's still the lens through which you see the world and interpret it. If you think that money is hard to come by, or that relationships will always end badly, then that's your story, and it's a self-fulfilling one that's on permanent repeat. As a result, patterns start to appear in your life – money becomes your pre-eminent struggle, or one bad relationship is followed by another.

But your story *isn't* true. If it were, nobody would be able to make money and every relationship would end badly, and there are plenty of examples in the world that contradict your story.

Often, though, the ways in which we define ourselves are more subtle, but are just as devastating on our lives. We may think we're not good enough, or that we don't deserve things – these were certainly two ideas about myself I carried around for years.

Your story isn't just a series of thoughts that are the aftertow of experiences. It has a deeper and richer resonance than mere thinking, although thoughts are one expression of your story (emotions are another, and a far more profound one). It goes deeper still, because what then sparks the emotion or the thought?

Footsteps through the generations

The rocket fuel of your story is an energy imprint from experience. This energy drives thoughts and emotions and provides the colour scheme to your world and the subtle hues that determine it.

This imprinting can sometimes move beyond an individual and into a family or a generation, like sedimentary layers. For example, sociologists have noted that a tendency to commit suicide runs through families, and parents whose own parents were alcoholics often are themselves addicts or have children who become addicts.

Similarly, those who were raised in a household afflicted by a parent with gambling problems will also display similar traits – or, again, their children will. The reality of the past will create the circumstances in their lives right now and will continue to do so until they wake up to the unconscious processes that are wrecking their lives and those of their children.

We can all recognize these patterns, whether their origins are from our own experiences or from a leitmotif of a family or close community, even if few of us understand how they happen. Biologists maintain that behavioural patterns are the result of genetics and the imprinting in our DNA, but the science of epigenetics – which studies outside influences on DNA coding – tells us that our environment, including the people in it, are more powerful influences and can overwrite genetic coding.

This energy does something far cleverer than just create your story, though – it creates 'you' in the process. A story without a central character wouldn't be much of a story, although you're the hero, the teller and the listener of yours. So, when we say that an abused person is drawn to more abuse in his life, the energy imprint of the experience of abuse itself seeks out more abuse.

'You' are created as a necessary part of that process. That you assumes the mantle of the thinker, and without you, the essential part of the process – the thought itself – would collapse under the logical absurdity of there being a thought without a thinker. Yet you've become so bewitched by the energy's drives that you're convinced you're a continuous and coherent 'I', sitting in command-central.

It feels that way, too. You think when you want to or need to – or you think you do. You don't, of course.

Thoughts come into your mind all the time – it's like a tap that won't turn off. This constant stream of thoughts and feelings gives the impression of a permanent 'you'. But here's what's actually happening:

The thought thinks the thinker.

I think I'm not good enough, say: I'm not good enough because of the experiences I've had, usually as a small child. Tragically, too many of us are actually told this by our parents, or our teachers, or friends. If parents are kind enough to point this out beforehand, as my father was, almost everything that we do thereafter will be a vindication of this judgement.

The hurt that becomes your world

But what did we actually *feel* in that moment when we were told we weren't good enough, or we weren't as good as our brother or sister? Enormous hurt – a throbbing, raw heart of hurt. And it's this hurt that persists as an energy imprint. If you doubt this, there are hundreds of studies that demonstrate how past hurts affect our health, and even our longevity, when we grow up. I give a few examples of these in chapter 4.

It's the hurt itself that lives on, although the hurt becomes more subtle over time and becomes the lens through which we see ourselves and the world, and our chances of success in it.

This hurt finds expression through our brain and body as thoughts and emotions. And this is the meanest trick of all: these thoughts and emotions create a 'you' as they rise up. You, as a subset of the original hurt, which is translated into a thought or emotion, then become the owner of that thought. So not only do you then think you're not good enough, you aren't good enough because there's no distinction between you and the thought.

This becomes the starting point of almost every therapy because you then go to the therapist to seek his or her help in ridding yourself of your anger, or your inability to cope, your depression or anxiety, or your feeling of worthlessness. It's what I call the 'therapy triangle': there's you, your problem and the therapist.

It seems that there's a central player – 'you' – who's an active, independent entity that wants to overcome negative feelings. Once clear of these problems, you, the central player, are then free and unburdened, and able to live a fuller and more fulfilling life.

Because we live by the idea that 'I' am a constant and continuous agent, we seek help, or work on ourselves – to make us a better person, or rid us of our phobias and personality issues. Although the therapist may achieve temporary or slight improvements, deep and transformative change will be difficult while there remains a you who owns the problem.

'I'm often angry,' as another example, should more accurately be expressed as 'There's often anger that creates a sense of me in the process.' When it's seen in that way, the impulse to be calmer comes from the anger energy itself, and is a continuation of the same process.

This doesn't mean you do nothing, and just put up with the angry outbursts; the action is in the seeing, with absolute clarity, the process itself. Once seen completely, it dissolves naturally – as my depression and feelings of worthlessness did for me – and what remains is a feeling of joy and delight that's beyond words.

Only when you finally see there was only ever the thought itself – that there never was a 'you' that wasn't good enough or was angry – can the possibility of true healing begin. Until you completely see the process of the past, you'll continue to believe there's a you that's in control, that thinks when it needs to.

But if you do believe that, this central commander isn't very consistent – another clue that perhaps the idea of a continuous self is a mirage. If you watch closely, you'll see many thoughts that stake a claim as the real 'you' during your day. One moment you're someone who loses his temper, the next you can be the very model of patience. Sometimes you're very friendly, and other times you don't want to talk.

Because you constantly change, you can see the mess it creates in your life. We fall in love, we fall out of love; we make money and then we struggle with money; we're happy and then we become depressed and so we take antidepressants, drugs or alcohol or all three; we love our job and then we hate the job and want to quit it. For the rest of the time, we have mood swings. Of course, circumstances can change, but often it's us who are changing, and constantly.

Far from there being a 'you' that's the architect of all this, it's as though we've been possessed by an entity over which we've almost no control. We have, of course, and it's the past. As we get older, and have more experiences, the here and now becomes less apparent. We become *time-heavy*.

The past can also have a psychosomatic effect. How many times have you felt your stomach knot up as you think about someone who's upset you? Does an event in the past still have the power to make you angry today? Bad things that happen to us as children can make us chronically ill when we're adults. The event doesn't have to be as severe as sexual molestation; it can be anything from a father who shouts at us, to a mother who's never at home when we come back from school.

Even though the parents may be dead, their power is such that they can reach out through time and give us a fatal heart attack. How could that happen, unless the past lives on in us as some energetic entity?

As the past grows, so we feel increasingly separate from the world. Our sense of a self – made up of past sufferings, sadness, regrets and disappointments – becomes a fortress against a world that's hostile and against us. As the past grows in us, so does a sense of space that separates us from the world.

The time machine

So what are you that you can live in the present and yet be more influenced by the past, which separates you from the world? You're a time machine: you create an imagined future from a past that you didn't completely understand in the first place. This continual time projection – from past to future – bypasses the present, and events in the present moment are invariably seen and interpreted through the filter of the past.

As a result, you never fully experience the moment, when any seeming division between you and the world would evaporate and the fortress walls of the self would melt.

As a self that's made up of the past, you're a complex mass of feelings and emotions that has the potential to blow like a volcano at any time. The trouble is that you don't know what may trigger an outburst. It could be the wrong word at the wrong time, a situation you encounter, even a toothpaste tube squeezed the wrong way.

You don't do it because you're a 'bad' person. Having angry outbursts or occasional emotional eruptions isn't an aspect of your inherent nature – it happens because the impulse from the past truly wants to understand.

> *This book will explain why it is we feel hurt and upset in the first place, where these feelings of hurt come from and what the whole process is trying to achieve. As you read it, you'll start to recognize an energetic impulse that seeks understanding through you as a body in time and space.*

While you're unaware of this movement, you're living unconsciously. You're often unconscious of the referencing, the projection from the past into a future, yet it colours your world every moment, and the more you're in the thrall of these waves of psychological time, the less happy you are.

Most thoughts and feelings have their origins in the past. These feelings are the accumulation of hurts, disappointments and upsets that have happened. That past may be just a few seconds old, as happens when we think about solving a problem that has just cropped up, but it's more often from years ago.

The past becomes a weight. Yet how does this affliction of time happen? How did the untrue story of you begin?

Your Three Selves

If the past is a 'body', or energy centre, and if you already have a physical body, this suggests you have more than one body. But you don't have two bodies, or selves – you have three. You may live in present time, while being more influenced by the past, but you also have experiences that seem to be outside of space and time.

These strange phenomena – the intuitive leap, the sense you just 'knew' something was going to happen, or the dream that foretells a future event – suggest that there's a third 'you' that's not dependent on time.

I call these three selves, or centres, the Present time-body, the Past time-body and the Potential centre. It might seem an extraordinary thought that you're the amalgam of three entities, each calling itself 'me' or 'I', but this isn't so alien a concept if you're from the Christian tradition. One of the axioms of Christianity is the idea of the three-in-one God: the Father, Son and Holy Ghost.

But Jesus's teachings were distorted. His original doctrine, espoused in the Gospels, stated that God is within us. Yet, within years of the establishment of the Christian Church, this radical idea was replaced by one that situated God in a distant Heaven, reached primarily through the intercessory powers of the priests.

The notion that we're made up of Three Selves is also not such a surprise to those of you immersed in ancient philosophy, especially that of Plato, who told us we are a blend of the intellect, passions and spirit.

The three-in-one self is also the basis of Freudian psychology, which proposes that we're made up of an ego, a subconscious and an unconscious, and the ancient wisdom schools often refer to the three bodies of the self – the gross body of the physical world, the subtle body of feelings and images, and the causal body of subtle energy.

So what's so special about my model? It's one of the first to explore who we are in and through time, a dimension that I believe is the key to our understanding. From this understanding we can achieve fulfilment, creativity and joy. Only when we clearly see ourselves as a creation of time and the past can we begin to live fully in the present moment – and lose our sense of separation, alienation and anguish.

Of the Three Selves in my model, the Past time-body causes most of our worries and, indeed, most of the strife in the world. It's the seat of both depression and addictions – as such, they have the same origins. It's where the past accumulates and the past-to-future movement occurs. As we grow older, the Past time-body has more energy from experiences and so becomes more substantial.

By the time we reach adulthood, we've become time-heavy. We're more past than present, whereas, when we're small children, we're time-light, more in the present moment than in the past. When the past doesn't dominate, there becomes less of a sense of space that separates us from the world and isolates us.

Do you remember when you were a small child – when you were time-light? You probably have some memories of that time, and they're likely to be idyllic (unless you were in an abusive family). Moments seemed to go on forever, and the slightest thing could fascinate you for hours. You felt at one with the world. It was your home, your playground, and any division between you and that world was slight. If you have small children yourself, their wonder at the world should remind you of how it is to be time-light and space-light.

Is that how you live your life every day now? I doubt it. Instead, it's likely that commitments and worries weigh you down, you're always planning for some imagined future, and you're concerned about money, your job, your family and children. It's natural to ensure you're secure – that you've enough food, proper shelter, and that you've good health – but is this supposed to take the joy out of your life?

Life for you today is invariably mundane, occasionally a struggle and, in the main, tolerable. You enjoy moments of happiness and joy, and reward yourself with the odd holiday, a nice meal, a bottle of wine or the latest movie. However, beneath this activity lies an undefined sense that life could and should be better, if only you knew how.

At this point, some of us get the 'spiritual bug' and desire enlightenment, bliss or nirvana, without recognizing that the very desire is merely a movement – from past unhappiness to an imagined joy in the future – that's the exact same as the one that covets the new Mercedes. As such, it becomes merely the latest chapter in your untrue story.

The metaphysical itch

Our tragedy is that, deep down, we do know that money or a big new house aren't quite going to hit the spot, that we've been locked out of an unspoken inheritance, a metaphysical right that came with our birth. Material success is a pale imitation of the glory that somehow should be ours. It's a little like the cosmic joke: 'Most of us go through life not knowing what we want, but feeling damned sure that this isn't it.'

You can get a sense of this by looking at your own life. Many of us live with a general sense of malaise, a greyness or fog that seems to have descended over the sun-filled days of our early childhood. We suffer anything from frequent irritation and regular angry outbursts to occasional stress, anxiety, phobias, or even chronic depression and finally to suicidal thoughts.

Many of us feature somewhere along this spectrum of desperate living. Life overwhelms one in five of us to such an extent that we regularly take a powerful antidepressant just to get through the day, and some one million people around the world commit suicide every year. Even if we eschew the antidepressant, many of us have various addictions – to alcohol, food, drugs, gambling, cigarettes or even sex.

So this becomes the story by which you live.

Chapter 3
You in the Now

*'Inside and outside are inseparable. The world is
wholly inside and I am wholly outside myself.'*

Maurice Merleau-Ponty

An ancient Vedic scripture marvelled that although
everyone dies, nobody seems to mind. It described the
phenomenon as one of the wonders of the world. Indeed it
is, because it would be rational for us to fear our death, our
absolute destruction, yet few, if any of us, actually do. Most of
us are embroiled in the rush of the daily round, and so we don't
have the time or inclination to ponder esoteric musings such
as the nature of the self and its relationship to time and space.

If we did, we'd probably recognize the current scientific model
– that the sense of a 'me' arises from the fact that there's a body.
This body lives through the dimensions of time and space, which
are independent of it, and you have little, if any, influence over
them. You and the world, therefore, are separate from each other.

Neuroscience would agree. According to current theory,
this sense of a 'me', which feels so substantial, is the result of
nothing more than a series of complex neural firings between
different areas of the brain.

Neuroscientists tell us that the human brain is made up of three parts: the old reptilian brain, which is concerned with survival, the mid-brain, which processes emotions, and the new brain, especially the pre-frontal cortex, where language, speech, reading and thinking all happen. This most recent development of the brain makes us human and separates us from the other animals, or so we like to tell ourselves.

Cumulatively, the sense of a substantial 'you' is as a ghost in the machine of the body, as the philosopher Gilbert Ryle once put it. When the body dies, the brain dies, and, with it, any sense of you. Similarly, if parts of the brain die, so parts of 'you' die, too, as we see in Alzheimer's or dementia patients.

If that model is correct, we return to our original Vedic question: why do you not fear your death? As I said, it would be rational to fear one's demise, so it could be because we're irrational. If we're merely neural firings, we don't have the imagination to fear our end, and if time and space are dimensions that are absolute and separate from us we don't have the capacity to grasp such an eventuality.

The Vedic question was, of course, a loaded one. We don't fear our death because 'we' don't die, even though every body does die, the Vedas tell us. If every body dies, then you aren't the body, and the 'real you' can't be an insubstantial phenomenon that arises from the brain's neural circuitry.

You and the world

The prevailing scientific model tells us that the sense of 'you' arises from the body, which is dependent on the ability to receive sensory data from the world. Therefore, we start with a world, then a body in the world, and finally a sense of you that arises from the brain's activities because of sensory data input. With this model, science has created a complete division between object (the world) and subject (you). The human race shall know the world through the rational mind and the sciences, and not through some mystical union with a world that we discern through magic, superstition and tea leaves in the bottom of a cup.

Here's the current view of the world and how the sense of a self arises:

World (time/space) ▸ **Body** ▸ **Self**

Although we're capable of amazing thought constructions, it all starts from the raw data from our senses. We wouldn't know, for example, that a hot radiator is hot until we touched it, or that lemons have a sour taste until we tasted one, or that a flower has a scent until we smelled a rose. We also fuse separate pieces of sense data, so we know a rose has thorns and that lemons have a rough skin.

By giving names to things in the world, we've constructed a language. From understanding number, space and elevation in space and time, we create a conceptual world of geometry, mathematics, and equations. Not only that, we can project our sense data into realms that don't even exist, and imagine golden horses or castles made of clouds.

Nevertheless, we can't imagine the golden horse if we've not already seen a horse and something made of gold. We can't envision a castle made from clouds if we don't know what both a castle and a cloud look like.

Even the mathematician wrestling with the most esoteric equations has to start with a world and sensory input, no matter how far his formulae may take him. There's no such thing as a brain in complete isolation from the world, and this brain thinks and rationalizes because of the sensory data it's constantly receiving.

This all seems like good common sense at first glance, but these supposedly firm foundations start to look a little shaky the deeper we dig. Are we really just a body with some cleverness thrown in? Our emotions and feelings suggest that we're something more.

Doctors are beginning to recognize the important role that our emotions play in determining our state of health and our recovery from disease. This emerging science, known as psychoneuroimmunology, already acknowledges that stress and emotions play an important role in inflammatory diseases such as arthritis[1] and that our level of self-esteem determines the health of our heart.[2]

Being happy and not worrying also dramatically reduces our chances of developing chronic heart failure. A study by Columbia University Medical Centre in New York, which involved 1,739 participants over a 10-year period, established that our attitudes towards life have a direct and powerful effect on the heart. Happy people who tend not to overly worry about things are far less likely to suffer heart problems than are their more gloomy counterparts.[3]

Women who've suffered recurrent episodes of breast cancer dramatically reduce the risk of a further bout just by learning a few skills to reduce their stress levels. In one experiment involving 227 women with breast cancer, those who were taught how to lower stress had a 45 per cent reduced risk of developing the cancer again, and they were cancer-free even 11 years afterwards.[4]

Positive thoughts really do aid wellness, just as negative ones make us ill. Consequently, the idea of the self as a simple, sensory-related phenomenon starts to get a little more complicated. Our sense of self in time can be changed by the way we *feel*.

The world through our senses

Can we entirely rely on our senses? Is my sense of 'red' the same as yours? Can we agree on what 'hotness' is? To illustrate this point, researchers have carried out experiments with a chemical called phenol-thio-urea. To most people, it has a bitter taste, but for around a quarter of those who've taken part in tasting experiments, it has no taste at all. So is the chemical bitter or not? Putting it another way, is the bitterness in the chemical, or in our senses?

The world we experience through our senses is not the same world that other living things see, hear and taste. Biologists have discovered that bees see a colour range beyond our visual capacity, that ants sense polarized light, that bats detect warmth from another living thing up to 16 cm (6 inches) away, that cats have a hearing range of between 100 and 60,000Hz, and that dolphins hear sounds up to at least 100,000Hz.

By comparison, our hearing range is a mere 20,000Hz. The lowest register we hear is at approximately 20Hz, whereas an elephant can hear a sound as low as 1Hz. The humble pig with its 15,000 taste buds can taste things that we can't detect with our 9,000, and the pig pales in comparison to the rabbit, which has 20,000 taste buds.

> *Our senses are not capable of telling us everything about the world that apparently sits outside of us. It has colours, sounds and tastes well beyond our sensual spectrum, yet the world for the bat and the bee is as real for them as ours is for us. So, what's real? Is there an absolute reality?*

The new sciences are also blurring the edges that apparently divide you from the world outside of your body. A new branch of biology known as epigenetics is challenging the theory that you're entirely the result of the genetic codes in your DNA. Epigeneticists now believe that our genes are switched on and off by atoms above the gene that are affected by our immediate environment: the food we eat, the pollutants we're exposed to and the level of stress we encounter.

Lars Olov Bygren, a specialist in preventive health at the Karolinska Institute in Stockholm, Sweden, researched the parish records of a remote town in the north of the country and discovered evidence of an environmental effect that has passed down through the generations.[5] A famine at key moments in the lives of grandparents directly affected the life expectancy of the grandchildren, irrespective of their genetic profile. Environmental factors have overwritten genetic code.

A similar situation occurred with women who were pregnant at the time of the 9/11 terror attack on the World Trade Center in New York. Psychologist Rachel Yehuda, at the

Mount Sinai School of Medicine in New York, has discovered that women who were either inside the building or close to it at the time when the attack occurred have passed on the effects of their stress to their children.[6]

Professor Wolf Reik at the Babraham Institute in Cambridge, UK, has demonstrated that the switches that control our genetic coding are themselves inherited, suggesting that a 'memory' of an event passes through the generations. As he says, genes and the environment are not mutually exclusive, but are inextricably intertwined, with one affecting the other. So if you're as much your environment as you are your DNA, where do you actually begin and end?

Darwin's theory of evolution also supports this blurring of the dividing line between body and world, subject and object. Evolutionists may make statements such as, 'Dinosaurs evolved into birds' or 'The hairy mammoth evolved into today's elephant,' but this isn't what actually happened. Dinosaurs were not self-willed agents that decided to become birds in order to survive; instead, the environment in particular, and life in general, changed the dinosaur.

As such, it changed to be the fittest for its environment; the immediate environment shapes you as much as your inherited DNA. You're not a set of predetermined pieces of genetic code on legs; you're also part of a dynamic world, which is as much you as you are it. While Darwin believed this process happens over millions of years, epigeneticists are demonstrating that DNA can be overwritten in a generation.

The cognitive philosopher Alva Noe, at the University of California at Berkeley, has demonstrated how the environment plays a key role in creating our sense of a self and our interior landscape. Our visual apparatus is a vital way for us to learn about the world around us – but Noe invites us to consider what would happen to someone who, for some reason, wasn't permitted to see as an infant.

Although it's difficult fully to comprehend the difference between the consciousness of someone deprived of sight and someone who's enjoyed full visual stimulation, the inability to see will affect the development of neural interconnections that are necessary for vision. Thus, in some way, the boy deprived of sight during the crucial years when his brain is developing will be different from the boy whose sight was not impaired. The environment, therefore, has affected the boy in Noe's thought experiment and has contributed to making him that which he's become.

Your innate connection with the world

We seem to have an innate knowledge of the world that goes beyond the data fed to us by our senses. For example, if I show you a colour chart with subtle and changing shades, you'll be able to detect if a shade is missing from the spectrum, even though you've never seen the chart before. Similarly, if you hear a range of several octaves, you'll know instantly if the musician doesn't play one of the notes.

Neuroscientists argue that these patterns are hardwired into our brain, but how did this happen, and where did the brain get the pattern from in the first place? The immediate answer to the latter question is to suggest that it comes from the world itself, but, of course, the response is circular. If that's the case, how did the brain know there was a missing colour or note in order for the evolutionary hardwiring to begin?

There are similar problems about our sense of beauty and morality. While both seem to be subject to change, fashion and social values, there's an essence to them that transcends time. I well remember taking our youngest daughter, when she was eight, to the Louvre Museum in Paris. As we turned a corner, the headless Winged Victory of Samothrace, carved more than 2,000 years ago, confronted us.

My daughter stopped in her tracks and looked in utter awe at the sculpture before her. 'It's beautiful,' she gasped. Of course it is, as hundreds of generations before us would agree, and, doubtlessly, as will the generations that follow. So what was it in my daughter, more familiar with images of pop stars, that could register beauty in an ancient statue that's missing vital parts?

The same goes for basic right and wrong. While morality changes with societal mores, our fundamental sense of rightness and fairness seems to run like a seam throughout history. Although most mothers have intervened to make their child share with another, researchers have also noticed that a sense of fairness, and of taking turns, is inherent in one-year-olds.

Yet where does such an abstract idea as rightness and turn-taking come from if we can't pick it up through our senses? Do we get it from the world, and if not, what is this mysterious osmosis that happens within months of our birth?

We have an intimate relationship with the world and to the events that happen in time and space. We're at home in the world. We know when the ground in front of us is substantial, and when we reach out for a piece of paper, we're confident that we'll be able to touch it. We can even predict events or assess that we can't cross the road safely because the car is travelling too fast, or know that we can catch the ball if we move a few steps to the right.

If we're ultimately sense-input beings, as the current scientific view suggests we are, there are only limited ways that we get information and knowledge. We can do so through an association of ideas – such as conjuring up that golden horse in our imagination or figuring out an equation – or from matters of fact, as the empirical philosopher David Hume made clear.

So how is it possible for us to have pre-existing patterns in our head that tell us a colour or a note is missing, that give us a universal sense of beauty, an inherent sense of right and wrong, and an ability to predict something we may never have seen before?

You create time and space

We can't answer these questions without coming up with an answer that takes us on an endless loop. What comes first? Us or the world? If it's us, how can we be affected and shaped by the world? If it's the world, how can we have an innate sense of right and wrong, colour and beauty?

One solution – mooted more than 200 years ago by the philosopher Immanuel Kant, after spending years pondering the very same issues – is that we ourselves impose the framework of time and space onto a canvas that, because it must have neither of those dimensions, is eternal and infinite. It's a brilliant solution, and one that solves the 'world knot' as Kant's disciple, Arthur Schopenhauer, described the relationship between us and the world.

The answer is that neither the world nor humanity came first, but both are inextricably codependent on the other. Without a body – and a brain that creates the matrix of time and space – there would be no world, and yet, in a symbiotic dance, our body is in the world of its own creation.

Kant was one of the first philosophers to try to explain consciousness – the elusive 'thing' that's more than merely a brain activity that allows us to have sensory experiences. As Kant demonstrated, consciousness is the ground of being that encompasses the world and us in a two-way supportive relationship.

Kant's revolutionary premise presaged the discoveries of quantum physics some 120 years later. He posited our central role in the co-creation of the world in time and space, and quantum physicists have demonstrated that there are no phenomena of 'stuff', or reality, until it's observed. In essence, the world comes into being in the very act of observing it.

A new scheme of the world and you:

The World ↑
The Body |
The Self ↓

The eminent quantum physicist Eugene Wigner remarked that consciousness was the only reality: 'It was not possible to formulate the laws of quantum mechanics in a fully consistent way without reference to the consciousness of the observer. The very study of the external world led to the conclusion that the content of consciousness is the ultimate reality.'

Wigner was one of the figureheads of a new branch of quantum physics that positions perception at the very heart of creation itself, just as Kant had concluded. However, there are paradoxes within the paradox: If Wigner is correct, am I dependent on others for my existence? Do others perceive me into being?

Quantum physics tells us that the phenomena of time and space occur only at the collapse of the wave function, when quantum particles 'solidify' into measurable matter. Nevertheless, scientists have argued about where the demarcation line occurs.

For Wigner and his followers, it must be at the moment of perception, as we freeze quantum particles into a specific time and space, and we need a continual regress of perception so that you – and I – can exist, a phenomenon he called 'Wigner's friend'. Wigner's friend perceives Wigner into being, who perceives his friends into being, ad infinitum. We're therefore creating and being created at every moment.

Kant, Wigner and others may not have fully appreciated the extent of the paradox. While I perceive the world into being, my body – and my brain, as the perceiving instrument – becomes part of its own creation. This suggests that the real perceiver is not my brain, or my body at all, which, in turn, means that I'm not my body, but ultimately that which sees my body into being.

No wonder we don't fear our death.

Summary

The prevailing view that the sense of an 'I' is created from the outside in – from the world, to a body, to a sense of you – rests on a circular argument in order to explain the special relationship we have with the world and how we know things beyond our sensory data. We can explain that special relationship – and get rid of the circularity – only if we see ourselves as co-creators of the world we inhabit, imposing time and space onto a canvas that's eternal and infinite.

We not only live in the present, we also create it. This special relationship dissolves the dividing line between my body and the world. I also influence the world around me through my thoughts and my feelings. Reality is not just something that happens to me – it's something that I co-create.

Chapter 4
You and the Past

'There is no present or future, only the past,
happening over and over again, now.'

Eugene O'Neill, *A Moon for the Misbegotten*

Every moment we are *experiencing*. We experience the sensation of the chair under our legs, the hum of the air-conditioning system, the taste of the coffee we've just drunk. These are primarily neutral experiences and they form the backdrop of our life. Most of these experiences pass through us, so to speak, and they make up the sensory data that tell us there's a world out there and that we're having an experience in it.

However, not all experiences are quite so neutral. Some go beyond pure sensory input and require your involvement as a being that thinks and feels. Let's say you unexpectedly bump into an acquaintance in the street – how do you respond? Almost inevitably, the past plays a part. If you know the person, it would seem strange and very antisocial to walk past without acknowledging him or her.

The meeting will also produce some quick shorthand about the person – even if you're not immediately conscious of it – telling you they are to be welcomed or avoided. The same goes for a problem you may need to solve. You'll call on your experience and any training and expertise you have in order to resolve it.

These are examples of when memory is a friend – when it helps you to navigate your way around the world. However, memory can also be less coherent or clear. Sometimes it's like a quick movement that you just glimpse out of the corner of your eye. This is the memory of past events and experiences, not always fully recalled, but which nonetheless has an energetic charge.

Often these memories are associated with a feeling of sadness, anger or fear. The sensation may be blurry or incomplete, and yet it sometimes even causes a psychosomatic reaction. Memories of an extreme experience, for example, can make the hands sweat or the heart palpitate as though it were happening to you right now.

Your map of thoughts

Experiences, or our memory of them, also give us an inexact reading of the world. Although there's a logical frame to these memories, the logic is that of a wonderland – a hermetically sealed universe where reality makes sense only within its own boundaries. Any experience leaves some trace or residue that creates a private world, and provides reference points for our interpretation of events.

These memories form our map of the world: the way it works and the qualities of the people in it. We usually never openly express these shadowy feelings about the world.

Although our map is real to us, the memories on which it's based are not true for several reasons:

- A memory is never an accurate representation of an event, but rather the emotional extraction from it – the sensation or feeling we've been left with.

- The memory isn't true because the experience itself was not true to begin with. Every experience has us at its centre, viewed from our own perspective. We can't experience the whole because, as sensory beings, we're not the whole.

- We're already limited by previous experience and by our position at a specific point in space and time. If we were a purely perceiving thing, we wouldn't have a memory of an experience at all. But we're not simple enough to just see, hear or touch – instead, we interpret through the filter of faulty and incomplete memory.

When I interact with you, I can't fully understand your perspective any more than I can see the complex interplay of events that led up to our experience. I can't see the web of life, the endless round of cause and effect that led to the moment when something happened in which I played a part.

As you try to pinpoint the moment when one cause has an effect, you'll soon discover that you're on an infinite regress, as an endless chain of previous events made possible the moment you're trying to comprehend. Something always precedes your current experience that has an influence on the present.

These half-formed, shadowy memories are not expressed as thoughts; they're *feelings*, an undefined *sense* of something. These feelings create your map – a filter through which you see the world and colour your experience.

This filter is the summation of experience, determining the way you react in the present, and how you see the world. It plays out every time you face a situation in the present moment that's reminiscent of a past event. It's the untrue story of you, and it tells you that you're undeserving, or angry, or a failure.

The filter permeates almost every part of you. You may have a sense that life is hard, people are ungrateful or your spouse doesn't understand you. These thoughts and almost every abstract thought like them have their foundations on nothing more substantial than feelings, which are the afterglow of a memory from a partially understood experience. These feelings may not be apparent, but they colour your world, which in turn becomes a reflection of your own thoughts, beliefs and attitudes.

A wonderful Zen story makes the point. A traveller was making his way to a town when he saw an old man sitting by the side of the road. 'What are the people like in the next town?' he asked the old man.

'How were the people in the town you've just left?' the old man responded.

'Oh, they were cold, indifferent and antisocial. That's why I left.'

'I'm afraid you'll find the people in the next town are just the same,' said the old man.

A few hours later, another traveller walked by, and asked the old man the same question.

'How are the people in the next town?' he asked.

Again, the old man responded, 'How were they in the last town?' The traveller told him the people were warm, friendly and helpful.

'They're just the same in the next town,' said the old man.

Feelings and mega-feelings

Your thoughts and feelings become apparent when something sets you off. It could be a word, a phrase, an action or a situation, but whatever the trigger, you suddenly react. Or it could be an explosion, an eruption often out of all proportion to the circumstance.

You also walk around with a range of concepts that I call mega-feelings, which are the accumulation of a range of experiences. These mega-feelings tell you that there's a substantial you and that there's a world 'out there'. However, as we saw in the previous chapter, this 'you' and a world 'out there' are not as clearly delineated as you assume. You don't really know who you are, any more than you know where you end and a world out there begins.

We'll explore these ideas in the second part of the book, when we'll look more closely at the past that seems to inhabit us. For now, it's enough to know that you're in its thrall, even though you may not be conscious of the constant past-to-present movement that defines and delineates your reality.

As you grow older and accumulate more experience, the filter itself strengthens. Eventually, the accumulated past forms your reality and takes on more meaning and significance than that which is in front of you right now. You don't realize that you're slowly becoming the past, yet many of your thoughts, responses and emotions have their basis in the past – your past.

The three types of experience

Experiences can be broadly categorized as having been good, bad or neutral. Neutral experiences – ones that don't leave an energetic print – are the most common. 'Bad' experiences from the past, which leave a trace of sadness, anger or fear, are often reinforced when something similar occurs in the present moment. There's a recognition, as if you see how a situation will play itself out, and the feelings – from incomplete and faulty memory – start to rise up.

Good experiences produce a sudden feeling of joy or unity – an oceanic feeling, as some psychologists describe it – when you feel complete and whole. These latter experiences are invariably the seed of addictive behaviour, as we seek to relive that sensation. We'll explore this process more fully in the second part of the book.

When we're very young, we delight in the moment, as the world unfolds to us. The slightest thing – a worm wriggling in the soil, a dandelion, a bird pecking for food – captivates us. If you have children or grandchildren and they're young enough, you can see this for yourself.

However, this golden age is soon over, and life, with its conflicts and troubles, quickly rushes in. Researchers at the Kaiser Permanente Hospital in San Diego, California, researching how childhood hurts affect us as adults, have come up with surprising conclusions.

The more abuse we suffered as a child – and, by abuse, the researchers include any sort of emotional and physical abuse – the shorter our lives. The way our parents treated us when we were children determines how long we'll live.

The research team drew up a list of 18 possible abuses, which they called 'adverse childhood experiences' (ACEs):

1. A parent swore at or insulted the child.

2. A parent acted in a way that made the child fear he or she might be physically harmed.

3. A parent often slapped, pushed or grabbed the child.

4. A parent often hit a child so hard that there were marks or injuries.

5. A parent touched or fondled the child.

6. A parent wanted the child to touch them in a sexual way.

7. A parent attempted some form of sexual intercourse with the child.

8. A parent succeeded in having sexual intercourse with the child.

9. A parent had a drink or substance abuse problem.

10. A parent used street drugs.

11. A parent was depressed or mentally ill.

12. A parent attempted suicide.

13. The mother was sometimes pushed or grabbed.

14. The mother was kicked, bitten or hit with a fist.

15. The mother was repeatedly hit.

16. The mother was threatened with a knife or gun.

17. A parent went to prison.

18. Parents were separated or divorced.

Of their sampling, approximately 12,000 of the 17,000 participants recorded at least one ACE from their childhood. Probably most of us would do the same. How many times did your parents insult you in some way when you were a child? How many times did they belittle you, or tell you that you weren't good enough?

As you'll see, we carry those hurts with us for all our days and eventually they could even kill us. As the researchers discovered, those participants who suffered six or more ACEs as children died 20 years before a participant who'd not recorded any ACEs. David Brown, the project leader, commented: 'It's important to understand that consequences to childhood trauma can extend over an individual's life'[1]

Another study, published around the same time, reached a similar conclusion. Researchers at King's College, London, tracked the lives of 1,037 participants from their birth in 1972 and 1973 into adulthood. During the first 10 years, the researchers noted any adverse experiences the participants might have endured, such as poverty, maltreatment or social isolation.

Those participants who suffered three such adverse events as children were more likely to be currently suffering from depression or inflammatory problems – often a precursor to heart disease, arthritis and the like – or already displayed other risk factors, such as high blood pressure, obesity or abnormal cholesterol levels. In fact, the research team reckons that 31 per cent of all cases of depression and 32 per cent of instances of high blood pressure or cholesterol levels are the direct result of an unhappy childhood.[2]

Childhood abuse of any sort brings on a host of physical diseases. Another study, this time of Jews living in Europe during World War II, found that those who were simply aware of the Holocaust – even if they didn't have direct experience of it – were far more likely to develop cancer than were Jews born after the war.[3]

In a separate study, researchers have discovered that people who experienced physical abuse as children run a far greater risk of developing osteoarthritis than those who had a happy childhood. The lead researcher, Esmé Fuller-Thomson from Canada's University of Toronto, said: 'This study provides further support for the need to investigate the possible role that childhood abuse plays in the development of chronic disease.'[4]

The past lives in us and through us. Even if it doesn't cause us physical harm, the past shapes our life. It gives us our picture of the world and the way it works. We live the life we reflect, and that reflection is from the past. It's our untrue story.

The past and the mirror

We either constantly relive our past or live a 'mirror pattern' of it, as I call it, in which we are driven to its opposite. A mother who forces her daughter to take ballet lessons because her own mother refused to allow her lessons when she was young is one typical example.

The woman who grieved

When her youngest child was about to head off to boarding school and a new life away from home, Helen Kirwan-Taylor recalls that she was 'on my knees with grief'. She was sobbing every night in the bathroom, and she was even thinking of leaving her husband, who'd insisted on boarding school for their child, and returning home to the USA.

Helen's sorrow was not for her departing son, however – as she discovered when she participated in a confrontational therapy technique known as the Hoffman Process. It was for her sister, who'd been brutally murdered 30 years earlier. For all those years, Helen had never come to terms with the terrible death of her sister. She'd been traumatized by the experience, yet there was no parallel experience in her ordered and happy life.

The event couldn't play itself out in Helen's life. Finally, an opportunity arose with the sudden loss of her son. This was the closest experience to the death of her sister that she could find in her life in order to undergo a process I call the 'displaced concept'. The feelings are the same, and yet everything else about the experience is changed, other than the central idea of loss.

A famous example of how the past haunts us and creates a mirror pattern comes from the life of the celebrated Victorian writer Charles Dickens. Dickens was 58 when he died at his home at Gad's Hill Place, in Higham, Kent, in 1870 – five days after suffering a stroke. He was one of the most famous authors of his age and has now taken his place in literature as one of the pre-eminent masters of fiction.

Although memorable comic characters and grotesques stride through all of his novels, Dickens's own childhood experiences feature most strongly. Most of his books have as a central character a child who's misunderstood, mistreated or in some way mishandled; often the child, who is born into poverty or becomes impoverished, turns out to be, at the very least, a saint or a martyr who dies in tragic circumstances.

In the use of children in his fiction, Dickens was often accused of being maudlin and sentimental. However, six years after his death, Dickens's official biographer, John Forster, revealed that the author had taken many of the incidents of childhood deprivation described in the books from his own life.

Dickens said his earliest years were idyllic, although he described himself as 'a very small and not-over-particularly-taken-care-of boy.' His memory of those times in the English coastal town of Portsmouth, where he was born, remained vivid; he claimed to have a photographic recall of the people and places of that time. The idyll was destroyed when Dickens was just 12 years old. His father was arrested and imprisoned at the Marshalsea debtor's prison after failing to pay his creditors.

Charles went to live in Camden, North London, with a family friend and started work at a blacking factory (which made the polish for boots). He worked 10 hours a day under conditions that would appal most of us today, long before the advent of child labour laws, trade unionism and workplace reform.

This experience would have a traumatic effect on him. Besides detailing the abuse of children strongly in his fiction, Dickens also spent the hours he was not writing working for the reform of living and labour conditions of the poor. Many of Dickens's friends were astonished at his prodigious energy; he would write all day, and then spend the night visiting the dives and dens around the London docks. He also produced plays and one-man shows, assuming the roles of some of the best-loved characters from his novels.

For all his life, Dickens feared the debtor's prison that was his father's home for several years. Within a short time of starting to write professionally, he'd earned enough money never to need to write another word, but his work rate remained phenomenal. He railed at requests for money from impoverished members of his own family, and even towards the end of his life, when his accumulated wealth was the equivalent of many tens of millions of pounds in today's terms, he still kept an eye open for other job opportunities or supplementary ways of earning an income.

Those close to Dickens believed that his work rate was a major factor in his premature death. He stuck to a gruelling tour of his one-man shows, and he collapsed and suffered a mild stroke after one of them, nearly a year before he died. However, Dickens didn't heed the warning signals, and carried on with his extraordinary work schedule. On the day he suffered the stroke that would prove fatal, five days later, he'd put in a full day's work on his final uncompleted novel, *The Mystery of Edwin Drood*.

Few of us have the genius or energy of Dickens, but most of us can empathize with the demons that haunted him, driving him on to an early death. Whether the patterns from the past are subtle or obvious, they'll form your reality.

As we saw with Kant, and with the quantum physicists, we play an essential role in the creation of the world, but so powerful is our focus that we create our personal world, too. So when you see through the eyes of the past, as if you were looking through a filter, you're bringing the past back to life in the present.

Your life does become tough, money does become hard to come by, keeping a job is always difficult – if that was how it used to be and you're unconscious of the movement from the past. Equally, if you've had an abusive husband in the past, you're more than likely to have one again until you wake up to the process and the patterns being created from your past. You've only two options: to remain unconscious or to wake up.

Dickens was driven by the feeling that life is hard and that money is always in short supply. He was haunted by the spectre of debt and the debtor's prison, even after he had accumulated a vast fortune. He may not have spent endless hours having such thoughts, but this was the filter through which he saw the world.

The past can be made up of experiences covering long durations of time, such as when Dickens's father was imprisoned for several years, but it's also formed from transitory sensations when something hurtful was said only once, or as a result of traumatic or 'difficult' experiences that happened infrequently. Irrespective of the duration of the event, the past seems to flatten down into a one-dimensional memory, like an energetic print permanently on repeat.

Several of the ACEs listed by the Kaiser Permanente researchers didn't mention duration; it was sufficient that a parent shouted at you just once or twice for it to be viewed by the researchers as an 'adverse event'. For a sensitive child, that event could go deep and live on for his entire life. Although the coroner's report stated that Dickens died from a stroke, in fact he died from a past that continued to live on – that became his never-changing present.

Summary

The past infests us. It shapes our reality every day. It becomes our reality. Although it's a very potent force, we're invariably unconscious of its movements and the way it affects us from moment to moment. It creates psychological time, as it shifts the past to a projected future.

Chapter 5
You Out of Time

'There is no birth, there is no death; there is no coming, there is no going; there is no same; there is no different; there is no permanent self, there is no annihilation. We only think there is.'

THICH NHAT HANH

Y ou are a creator. You create the dimensions of time and space, and you create your reality by allowing the past to live through you. There's also an aspect of you that's outside both time and space, and you bring this into the world, too. We've all had that sudden feeling about a place or a person when something doesn't quite feel right, or when we feel immediate warmth, as if we're 'at home'.

Physicists are beginning to recognize the intuitive sense of already knowing an experience that's still unfolding as something that originates outside of space and time. How could familiarity with a completely new experience be otherwise?

We don't always have this strange sense of precognition when we're awake, although we may feel that something isn't quite right. Most often, a foreboding or presentiment of a future event happens when we're asleep. On the rare occasions when we recall our dreams, we sometimes recognize that the images in them foretell the future.

My own experience of this phenomenon happened just before the start of the football World Cup of 2010. I enjoy soccer, but my life is not changed by who wins or loses. I certainly don't lose sleep over it – although, three days before the tournament began, I did. I awoke with a start – around five in the morning, after vividly seeing that England would concede a simple goal through a stupid goalkeeping error.

I clearly saw the goalkeeper go down for the ball, which rolled under his body, and in his efforts to retrieve it he pushed it further across the line and into the goal. I also 'saw' that the score was one-nil to England's opponents, the USA, and that the goal happened in the second half.

The following day, I told five people about my dream, adding that if it turned out to be correct, they'd know that dreams could foretell the future. On the following Saturday, I settled down to watch the match, and, within five minutes, England had scored. So much for dreams foretelling the future, I thought.

Then, in the fortieth minute, one of the USA's players hit a long-range, speculative shot at goal. The England goalkeeper got himself behind the ball and then fumbled it, before it went under his body and he pushed it over the line. It happened just as I saw it in the dream! I was wrong about the score and the time of the goal – but the match-defining event happened as if it had been a film on repeat.

Things that happen outside space and time

My dream of a future event is fairly common. In 1927, Irish aeronautical engineer and researcher John (J.W.) Dunne wrote the classic work *An Experiment with Time* (Faber & Faber, London), the result of a study in which he recorded the number of premonitions experienced by a group of participants while they slept.

Dunne had trained his recruits to recall their dreams by following back the thought they had the moment they awoke and immediately writing it down. As they practised, they got better and better at remembering their dreams. During his research, Dunne discovered that dreams could foretell future events, often in vivid and precise detail, just as I'd experienced.

Dunne's underlying ambition with his study was to demonstrate that the concept of serial time – one moment following another – is a poor approximation of the truth. For Dunne, all of time is one vast canvas of now. Our human limitations prevent us from seeing the totality. It could be likened to a book; although the book is there in its entirety, we can take in only one page at a time, and usually sequentially by first reading page 20 before turning to page 21.

Nonetheless, page 1 and page 427 are also there at the same time, even though our focus may not be on either of them. Dunne believed that when we sleep, our perception alters, and, in a sense, we can see ahead to page 427.

Many of us have had similar experiences when there's a sudden upset in the expected sequence of serial time, and events don't follow their natural course as predicted by the laws of cause and effect. We might be thinking of someone moments before they telephone, sense that someone is looking at us although our head is turned, or have a premonition.

These examples could be dismissed as coincidence, wishful thinking or even the result of an overactive imagination were it not for the vast body of research clearly demonstrating instances when we *are* out of time and space. Here are some documented examples:

Moments of genius

These sudden flashes of inspiration can be so radical that they push the whole world in a completely new direction. Although they usually happen following a period of intense work and thought, these revolutionary insights are rarely the obvious conclusion of the thought processes that preceded them, or of sustained logical deduction. Instead, radical shifts in scientific thought are often the result of a flash of genius, and the progress of science is as much due to the sudden eureka moment as it is to methodical work.

Albert Einstein was a patent clerk, with the hope of promotion to Technical Expert, Second Class, when he had his flash of genius. He was travelling home in a crowded streetcar that was making its way through the busy streets of Bern, Switzerland, one evening in 1904. As it passed the city's famous medieval clock tower, the Zytglogge, the young Einstein suddenly had the realization that time is not an absolute, as Sir Isaac Newton had asserted, but was relative to the position of the observer and to the speed at which he was travelling.

A year later, Einstein published a short paper that mathematically demonstrated this radical idea – which he called the Theory of Special Relativity – along with two other remarkable papers, one of which was to win him the Nobel Prize. Einstein's paradigm-shifting insights ushered in the strange world of quantum physics, which would extend his insight and establish the observer as the determining factor in fixing reality.

Einstein was certainly not alone in having such paradigm-shifting insights. In 1843, Sir William Rowan Hamilton, a professor of mathematics and astronomy at the University of Dublin in Ireland, was walking across the city's Brougham Bridge when he suddenly 'saw' in its entirety his Quaternion Theory, which would transform modern mechanics. In that same moment he also realized it would take a further 15 years to work out the details of this instantaneous vision.

The Serbian-American inventor Nikola Tesla, one of the great geniuses of science, suddenly came up with the idea for alternating current while he was out walking and quoting a passage from Goethe's *Faust*. The German-American pharmacologist Otto Loewi claimed to have dreamed how nerve impulses were transmitted chemically, and not electronically, as was then the prevailing view.

Loewi said he dreamed the solution, awoke in the middle of the night, hurriedly scribbled down his discovery, and then went back to sleep. The next morning he went to read his notes, and could not make head or tail of the illegible scribbles. That night he had the same dream, and this time when he awoke he wrote more carefully.

Artists, too, are renowned for moments of genius, when they somehow grasp wonderfully inspiring sounds, words, and images from a place beyond time and space. Beethoven often mentioned in his notebooks that he was transcribing from nature, and that if he didn't write down the notes he was hearing, he was sure that someone else eventually would. The Ninth Symphony was not his creation, he claimed, but was already a completed work in the ether, waiting to be transcribed.

Near-death experiences

A US Gallup poll has estimated that up to 12 million Americans have had some experience of life after death, but are too embarrassed to admit to it.

One interesting instance concerned the philosopher A.J. 'Freddie' Ayer, whose own rigorous logic would have dismissed claims of an afterlife – until it happened to him. In 1988, when he was 78 years old, Ayer's mental capacities were as sharp as ever, and he was still very much in the business of not taking intellectual prisoners with his no-nonsense rationalism. However, his body was weakening, and he suffered a severe bout of pneumonia while in the United States.

He spent 10 days in a hospital in New York before flying home to England, where he immediately resumed his hectic social life. 'Retribution struck me on Sunday, May 30,' he related in an article for the *National Review* published on 14 October 1988. 'I had gone out to lunch, had a great deal to eat and drink, and chattered incessantly. That evening I had a relapse. I could eat almost none of the food which a friend had brought to cook in my house.'

Worse was to follow. The next day, Ayer had a long-standing engagement for lunch with a friend, and after making his way home, he went straight to bed. The following day, when his health had worsened even further, he was taken to University College Hospital in London, put into the intensive care unit, and tended by a young doctor who'd been an undergraduate at New College, Oxford, when Ayer had been a lecturer there.

'He was so much in awe of me that he forbade me to be disturbed at night, even when the experienced sister and nurse believed it to be necessary,' recounted Ayer in his typical immodest way.

Ayer started to recover, but always declined the hospital's food. Used to the better things in life, he was brought fine foods by friends and admirers. One evening, he 'carelessly tossed' a slice of smoked salmon into his mouth. It went down the wrong way, and almost immediately, his heart slowed before stopping completely. He was dead for four minutes while the emergency staff worked frantically to save the life of their most famous patient.

They were successful, and Ayer jolted back to life. The very first words he uttered were, 'You are all mad.' Ayer said he didn't know why he'd said such a thing, but a few hours later, he told a visitor that while he was 'dead' he'd seen a bright red light. 'I was aware that this light was responsible for the government of the universe,' he wrote.

In his *National Review* article, Ayer said that his experiences were 'rather strong evidence that death does not put an end to consciousness' and that they 'slightly weakened my conviction that my genuine death will be the end of me, though I continue to hope that it will be'. The experience certainly seemed to have mellowed the usually acerbic Ayer; as his wife noted, 'Freddie has been so much nicer since he died.'

Ayer did indeed die 13 months later, in June 1989, but there remained one final mystery. It seems that he did not apply his usual rigorous standards to the account of his near-death experience (NDE) given to friends and the readers of the *National Review*.

Years later, the young doctor who'd attended Ayer, Dr Jeremy George, revealed that the philosopher had disclosed that he'd seen the 'supreme being' during his four minutes in the death state. 'I'm afraid I'm going to have to revise all my books and opinions,' he'd apparently added. This was something that Ayer had never recounted to anyone else. To do so would have thrown into question his life-long philosophical stance.

Neuroscientists dismiss near-death experiences as the result of over-activity in a brain starved of oxygen. However, many cases of NDEs happen to patients who are completely devoid of any physical and mental activity and so are clinically dead.

The starved-brain theory also can't explain the many cases of 'dead' patients who continue to observe exactly what's happening in the emergency room and can relate the sequence of events in precise detail after they've been revived. In one case, a patient who 'saw' the nurse remove his dentures when he was clinically dead was able to remind her where she'd put them after he'd been jolted back to life.

Life-support patients

Patients who are clinically dead and need life-support in order to keep their organs functioning often retain a degree of consciousness. A study by Cambridge University in the UK discovered that a patient on life-support continues learning. In a simple experiment, the researchers played a tone immediately before blowing air into the patient's eye.

After doing this several times, the research team noticed that the patient would start to blink in anticipation of the puff of air when he heard the tone. This experiment demonstrates that even a patient in a vegetative state has a memory and learns to anticipate events.[1]

Spontaneous remission

Most diseases develop through a series of recognized stages. Cancer, for example, has four phases, and orthodox medicine maintains that it'll invariably result in death unless the patient is successfully treated. However, cancer specialists accept that some cases will spontaneously regress, which means the tumours mysteriously disappear. Nobody knows how common spontaneous remission is, although Professor Uwe Hobohm of the University of Applied Sciences in Giessen, Germany, reckons it may occur in one out of every 10,000 cases of cancer.

Researchers in Ontario, Canada, suggest that Hobohm has underestimated the rate. In their study, 145 cancer patients out of approximately 10,000 reviewed had had no medical treatment whatsoever. Of those, 35 per cent were alive five years later, and the average survival rate was 47 months. In addition, 70 per cent of those whose cancer didn't spread were living five years later. The overall survival rate among women was 45 per cent and, among men, 36 per cent.[2]

Whatever the true rate of spontaneous remission, the numbers are inevitably low in any study because the phenomenon is so hard to prove. Virtually all cases of cancer are treated by chemotherapy, radiotherapy or surgery – and an instance of spontaneous remission is considered valid only if there's been no medical intervention whatsoever.

Instances of spontaneous remission tend to be noticed only in those rare cases when the patient doesn't report the cancer until it's too advanced for medical intervention, and the patient, sent home to die, instead recovers. The event is also grossly under-reported because the patient usually doesn't get back in touch with the oncologist. If he does, the doctor doesn't record the recovery, usually because he doesn't believe it.

Remote viewing

Remote viewing is the ability to 'see' places or things that are far away or hidden from view. The remote viewer is usually given just a map or grid reference, and he uses it to zero in on the location and 'see' it. The CIA experimented with remote viewing during the Cold War, and researchers at the Princeton Engineering Anomalies Research (PEAR) laboratory in the USA have systematically studied it through 336 formal trials, invariably using a method they called 'precognitive remote perception'.

The remote viewer, seated in the PEAR laboratory, would be asked not only to name the destination of a fellow participant, but also to do so hours – and sometimes days – before his partner arrived, and often before the partner himself knew where he was going. In one case of precognitive viewing, the viewer described and drew a train station that the other participant would visit 35 minutes later.

In another example, the viewer had the 'strange but persistent' image of the other participant standing in a large bowl. Forty-five minutes later, the participant arrived at the massive domelike structure of the radio telescope in Kitt Peak, Arizona.

Other scientists have demonstrated in a variety of studies that people have the ability to see into the future. The late parapsychologist Charles Honorton, of the Maimonides Medical Center in Brooklyn, New York, carried out a meta-analysis of studies of 'future viewing', which usually involved predicting the symbols on a card or the numbers that would be thrown with dice. The combined result of 309 trials, involving approximately 2 million separate tests, was so robustly positive that the likelihood that they could have occurred by chance were 10 million billion billion to one.[3]

Telepathy

The psychologist Stanley Krippner, professor of psychology at Saybrook Graduate School, San Francisco, and the psychiatrist Montague Ullman, who founded the Dream Laboratory at the Maimonides Medical Center in New York, carried out a series of experiments demonstrating that thoughts could be transmitted by one volunteer to a sleeping participant, who would incorporate the ideas or images of the transmitted thought into his dreams. Researchers at the University of California independently corroborated the results, recording an 84 per cent accuracy rate. The odds for that level of success occurring by chance alone were 250,000 to one.

The man who should have died

The journalist Robert Blair Kaiser, a war reporter in Vietnam, and a former correspondent with Time *magazine and* Newsweek, *was behind the wheel of his car, pulling out of his driveway. Suddenly, as he said later, 'I was awakened from my dreamy preoccupation by the sight of a speeding car bearing down on me, not 5 feet (1.5 m) away on my left. I knew I was a dead man.*

'All of a sudden, that car was on my right… there was no way he could have missed crashing into me, no way he could have steered aside. His car had flashed through my car, his steel and glass and rubber passing through my steel and glass and rubber like a ray of light through a pane of alabaster.'[4]

According to natural laws, the two cars should have collided, as one car was travelling at speed and was a very short distance away when Kaiser saw it approaching. Yet it didn't happen.

Premonitions

The researchers Cassandra Eason, Sylvia Browne and others have investigated the bond that seems to exist between mothers and children, which doesn't appear to be dependent on time or space. Eason recalls one story of a young mother who left her small child for the first time with a babysitter to go to the cinema with her husband.

After a short while, she told her husband that she could smell smoke and that their baby was in danger. The husband tried to placate her, believing her fears were just those of an overanxious mother. However, the woman was insistent, so the couple abandoned the movie and rushed home – to discover a fire that had started in a downstairs room, the babysitter asleep, and the baby's room full of smoke.[5]

The holistic doctor and author Larry Dossey tells a similar story concerning a woman called Amanda. She'd dreamed that the chandelier in the next room had fallen from the ceiling onto her sleeping infant's crib and crushed the baby. In the dream, she observed that a clock in the baby's room read 4:35 a.m. and the wind and rain were hammering against the windows at the time the chandelier had crashed.

Extremely upset, Amanda woke up her husband and told him her dream. He insisted that it was meaningless and urged her to go back to sleep. However, the dream was so vivid and frightening that Amanda went into the baby's bedroom and brought the sleeping baby into their bed.

Soon she was woken up by a loud crash in the baby's room. She rushed in to see that the chandelier had fallen and crushed the crib – that the clock in the room read 4:35, and that wind and rain were howling outside. Her dream premonition was camera-like in detail, taking in the specific event, the precise time, and even a change in the weather.[6]

Dean Radin, senior scientist at the Institute of Noetic Sciences in Petaluma, California, who has tested thousands of cases of what he calls 'presentiments', believes that the experience is relatively common. He began researching the phenomenon in the 1980s after a friend told him a remarkable story.

The friend would always leave the sixth chamber of his gun empty while he was cleaning it, but on one occasion he had the overwhelming feeling that he shouldn't put the bullet back in the chamber afterwards. Several weeks later, he was in a drunken argument with his father-in-law, who suddenly reached for the gun. If the bullet had been in the chamber, Radin's friend would have died that day.[7]

Out-of-body experiences (OBEs)

The late sociologist and author Ian Currie, former professor of York University in Toronto, Canada, discovered that approximately 20 per cent of people have experienced the phenomenon of looking down at their own body from an aerial perspective.

In one case of a woman who claimed to have frequent out-of-body experiences, researchers placed a number on a small piece of paper in a script so small it could be read only if someone were centimetres away. The piece of paper was stuck to the ceiling, some 3.5 metres (12 feet) from the bed where she lay. She was monitored throughout the night while she slept, and, although she never left the bed, in the morning she was always able to tell the researchers the number they'd put on the ceiling.[8]

Reincarnation

The late Ian Stevenson, a former professor of psychiatry at the University of Virginia in the USA, put his academic standing at risk by carrying out exhaustive research into reincarnation, investigating thousands of cases over 40 years. In every instance, he explored alternative possibilities before deciding if the case could be explained only by reincarnation.

In one case, a boy in Beirut, Lebanon, recalled being a 25-year-old mechanic who'd been knocked down and killed some years previously. The boy knew the names of his sisters, parents and cousins in this earlier life – and even the name of the driver who'd knocked him down. The details identically matched an accident that had happened years before the boy was born, to a family unknown to him.

Stevenson explored the case further and was satisfied that he was not the victim of fraud and that the boy was not lying or mistaken. Eventually the case joined the 3,000 others that Stevenson had conservatively categorized as 'cases suggestive of reincarnation' and 'cases of the reincarnation type'.

I call these phenomena ESTs (Events outside Space and Time). From all of this evidence it seems indisputable that people have the potential to have experiences outside of serial time and their immediate space. Sometimes the law of cause and effect is violated, and events happen out of sequence. When they do, we call them miracles.

Despite the voluminous amount of research and evidence that supports ESTs, sceptics still doubt that they actually happen and dismiss them as cases of fraud, suggestion, or self-delusion, or as so trivial as to merit discounting. The paranormal researcher Michael Schmicker calls this approach 'scientism', which he describes as 'a philosophy of materialism, masquerading as scientific truth.'

He adds: 'Paranormal research has used the process of science to prove the existence of a variety of phenomena that simply doesn't fit within scientism's philosophy of materialism. If evidence conflicts with the philosophy, the evidence shouldn't be dismissed; instead, the philosophy should be revised.'[9]

Psychologist William James put it another way. It takes only one white crow to disprove the notion that all crows are black. Similarly, it takes just one legitimate case of EST from the many thousands collated to demonstrate that we're not always trapped in a determined universe of space and time. In my view, this has been proven beyond any doubt.

Two women who were healed by a miracle

Events outside Space and Time (ESTs) violate one or more of the natural laws, and they happen every day and to almost everyone at some time or another, even to me. My own EST concerned my mother, Edie, who at the time was aged 78. I was visiting her and my father one Sunday when someone accidentally brushed against her breast while walking past her. She immediately bent double, clearly in enormous pain. She confessed that she'd been nursing her breast for nearly two years, wrapping it in bandages, and hoping the open sores would just go away.

The rest of my family and I insisted she see the family doctor the following day, which she reluctantly agreed to do. According to her account, she said she'd never seen a doctor react in such a way before. When she'd shown him her breast, all he could see was an open red sore, which had enveloped the entire breast, and he recoiled in disgust and horror.

This was breast cancer in its final stages, and he confided to my father that she had, at most, three months to live. I was not prepared to accept that prognosis. I'd been the publisher of a health journal called What Doctors Don't Tell You, *and I knew there were many proven healing modalities that just might work.*

Within a week, we'd booked an appointment with a qualified doctor who, nonetheless, was pioneering alternative cancer therapies. He examined my mother's breast, and he, too, confirmed that this was cancer in its final stages. He immediately put my mother on a drip, which was delivering very high levels of hydrogen peroxide, vitamin C and other nutrients intravenously. He also insisted on a radical change of diet.

My mother dutifully travelled the 100 km (63 miles) to his surgery twice a week for her infusion, and slowly over the months the breast started to heal. Six months later the family doctor bumped into her in the street and genuinely thought he'd seen a ghost. He couldn't believe his eyes, and like most people who can't believe the evidence in front of them, he insisted on tests. My mother subjected herself to a mammogram that revealed that, indeed, the breast was completely free of cancer.

So did the vitamin C and hydrogen peroxide mix kill the cancer? Clearly so. However, something else also happened. When we first were given the diagnosis and prognosis, everyone in the family expressed their enormous love for Edie; as she was a woman who'd selflessly given all her life, these declarations were nothing less than the truth. For the first time, I 'love bombed' my mother with messages and flowers.

My father, who enjoyed spending money about as much as a banker relishes a zero-bonus year, suddenly raided his savings and willingly paid for all the expensive treatments. This was the highest expression of love my mother had ever witnessed.

The esteemed child-development researcher Joseph Chilton Pierce reported a similar experience. In his landmark book The Crack in the Cosmic Egg *(Park Street Press, 2002), Pierce revealed how his own wife succumbed to breast cancer, just as almost every female relative had before her. Despite the close attention of oncologists, his wife was given weeks to live, after nearly every vital organ had been removed, burned or permanently harmed.*

Like me, Pierce was also not prepared to accept the prognosis, and he spent night and day whispering positive and healing words to his comatose wife, who'd been sent home to die. This was an epic labour of love, and at the end, Pierce must have been utterly exhausted, having denied himself proper sleep or food for three weeks. However, the prize was beyond value. His wife started to make a full recovery, as though she'd been reprogrammed by Pierce's confident and positive code to be well.

Summary

Although you create time and space, you also live outside of both. This is the third, and final, element that makes you 'you'. It's also the most mysterious, because it throws up intriguing metaphysical questions about what it is that you are, whether you survive death and whether we're purely the body, subject to inevitable ageing and illness.

Although extreme examples don't happen to everyone, all of us have known moments that seem to occur when the laws of time or space, or those of both, are violated. This self that lives outside of space-time is also the creative impulse, as we've seen in instances of intuitive leaps and genius.

Chapter 6
You and Time

*'Man is an animal suspended in webs of
significance he himself has spun.'*

Clifford Geertz

As we've learned, neuroscience tells us that any sense of
an 'I' is the result of complex neural firings in the brain.
According to this view, the sense of self may seem substantial
and unchanging, yet it's fragile, a phantom that can be altered
through illness, brain injury, and ageing. When the body dies,
the brain dies with it. As a result, you die, too, as does everything
you thought you were.

Underpinning this is the belief that you are simply a body.
The sense of an 'I' comes from the workings of the brain, which,
in turn, is in the body. It would be reasonable to suppose, in that
case, that we'd do everything in our power to preserve and
protect the body. The principal role of the 'I' would be as the
body's guardian.

This doesn't always happen, as we see with people who are
drug addicts, alcoholics or smokers. Something in them seems
to turn against the wellbeing of the body, and appears intent on
either actively destroying it, or on satisfying a need that's greater

than its preservation. We're also prepared to sacrifice our body for a greater cause, such as in time of war or for a religious belief. This, too, suggests that we're more than a body.

On a more mundane level, we see contradictions in the way people behave. We often say one thing, but privately believe another. We contradict ourselves or constantly change our mind. We suffer from stress and anxiety, which suggests there are different aspects of the self, between which there are tensions and competing demands. For example, we can become stressed or anxious if we're doing one thing, but wanting to do another.

Who are you?

Our investigations also indicate you are more than one thing. Kant showed us that we have a special relationship with the world and that it's we – whoever 'we' are – who make the world what it is. Einstein and his discoveries took this further, ushering in the world of quantum physics and the primacy of the observer as the co-creator of his world.

With the help of a piece of smoked salmon, we also found that we appear to extend beyond space and time, and even to survive death. Charles Dickens, and the thousands who've taken part in important research projects into adverse events in childhood, coloured in the rest of the story of you by demonstrating the importance of the past in defining who it is that we think we are, the world we live in and what we perceive as reality.

So here's a quick résumé:

'You' can't be one thing

Most neurologists and biologists agree that we're only one thing: a body. Yet, if this were so, Professor Ayer couldn't have been both dead in his hospital bed and at the same time capable of registering a light, any more than other dead patients float above the bed and afterwards are able to recount exactly what was said and done while emergency crews were working on their bodies.

Similarly, you can't be just a body and, at the same time, be capable of influencing something thousands of kilometres away, just with your thoughts. Moreover, if you're only a brain and its appendages, how are you aware of visitors and their conversations, or able to learn simple skills, when your brain is comatose?

You're not always governed by time and space

Although it appears that we exist in a universe where time moves forward serially and space exists as an objective dimension, many instances suggest this isn't always the case. Every EST (Event outside Space and Time) – including premonitions, forebodings, and remote viewing – flouts the laws of time or space, or both.

The laws of cause and effect don't always govern you

A constant and immutable law of science is that every cause has an effect. Nevertheless, the myriad of examples of ESTs that we've already examined suggest that these laws can be violated.

We have a special relationship with the world

Kant was one of the first to realize that the world is relative to us. His early insight has since been supported by innumerable studies in the field of quantum physics. So special is this relationship, in fact, that it's difficult to say where 'you' end and the world 'outside' begins, as the science of epigenetics is discovering. This special relationship explains why we're able to have intuitive leaps and make extraordinary discoveries about the world that are not apparent to our senses.

We're co-creators of our reality

Quantum physics has demonstrated that we imprint time and space on the unknown, the infinite, and the eternal. We also create our own reality through our past, as happened to Charles Dickens and indeed happens to almost every one of us.

We're as much the past as we are the present

We're governed as much by the past as we are by the present – in many cases, more so. This past makes itself apparent through feelings we have, even though they're rarely perceptible to us. Feelings are also the building blocks of the concepts we have about the world and ourselves.

Every available explanation fails to capture the full richness of who we are, and no one definition explains the range of phenomena that we experience as human beings. All along, I believe the problem has been in looking for just one definition of the self. As long as we do so, we're never going to come up with an answer that satisfies all experiences associated with the self.

Philosophers have never been able to agree on what it is that we are:

- Plato said we're essentially a soul.

- Aristotle posited that we're a body without a soul.

- John Locke concluded that any sense of self comes from memory.

- Descartes claimed that we're a thinking thing that's separate from the body and survives death.

- David Hume outlined that the self is merely an agglomeration of sensual inputs.

- Spinoza surmised that we're a part of nature.

- Schopenhauer explained that we're a blind will to live.

- Nietzsche argued that we're a will to power.

...and so on throughout the centuries. Paradoxically, all of them were correct, in part, but ultimately they were wrong – because we're not just one thing. Clearly, we're more than what we're taught. There's more going on in us than merely a brain in a body.

Summary

People who hold to a sceptical and materialistic viewpoint often do so only by ignoring the evidence that contradicts their views. When all the evidence is included, and considered with an open mind, it's apparent that we're highly complex, with experiences in time and out of time, and yet defined by past time.

Part II

YOUR THREE SELVES

Chapter 7
The Three Time-Bodies

'Mass and energy are both but different
manifestations of the same thing – a somewhat
unfamiliar conception for the average mind.'

ALBERT EINSTEIN

You and your untrue story are the sum of Three Selves, or energy centres. Although each of these centres has its own vibrational pattern, there's overlap between all three, and the boundaries are fluid while the body is alive.

As an energy centre, each sends out a *pulse*, and the dominant pulse determines who you are at any one time. You could be fully present in the moment or thinking and worrying about the past – as increasingly happens as you age and become more time-heavy – or have a sudden uprush of joy and a feeling of unity with everything.

Neuroscience might suggest that these selves are merely the three parts of the physical brain. It's important to stress that my model is an energetic one, not a physical description. Energy is the ultimate reality of the universe, as Albert Einstein famously demonstrated, and the physical universe is merely energy that we sense.

It may be that the three-part brain is the physical apparatus through which the energetic one expresses itself, but this doesn't concern us. We must move beyond the physical – materialist – description, which has assumed that, by identifying and naming specific parts in the world, it can explain the mystery of you and the richness of the human experience. This approach to understanding is as satisfying and meaningful as attempting to learn about the beauty of music through the diagram of a violin.

Here's an overview of the Three Selves:

The Present time-body

The first of your Three Selves relates to the body and the world, and to living in time and space. Everything in the world – other people, the flora and fauna, our sun and the stars, the buildings, the cars – is within the Present time-body, as are you as a body and a brain.

It's strange to realize that the universe is a self. It's not your self, however, but the universal self that's expressing itself in and through each and every body. This process creates a feeling of a personal experience, which includes me – as an undefined entity – my body and, by extension, my possessions. This self creates time and space – and finds itself in it as a player in a drama that it's written, produced and staged (and observed as the audience).

It also completely identifies with its own creation. Indeed, it so much believes in its creation that it sees itself as separate and its body as different to all the other bodies it sees around it. You get a sense of this total immersion if you've ever been to a movie and become so engrossed in it that you forget yourself and enter the drama on the screen.

Actually, you're doing that every moment of your life, and you've forgotten that, with the Potential centre (see below) you're both infinite and limited by space, eternal and mortal, endlessly creative and restricted, completely free and a being caught in the web of cause and effect. Where 'you' are is determined by the dominant time-body or centre that creates your sense of self at any time.

The Present time-body is the centre that's most understood by the sciences, including physics, astrophysics, biology, and medicine, and it deals with the world of concepts, of things and stuff, of the measurable and definable. The Present time-body also includes the intangible – our fears, anger, rage, hunger, thirst, and sexual desire in the moment – which continues to reverberate within it as an emotional footprint. Just as a dog might be fearful of other dogs after a savage attack, so the Present time-body carries a resonance of a previous experience.

However, as we saw in Part I, we're more than the present moment; we're as much the past as we are the 'now', and it's the past that shapes us and our world, motivates us, makes us go to war, and may even eventually kill us.

The Past time-body

This is the second of your Three Selves, and it's the one that's primarily responsible for your untrue story. It stands between 'you' and a rich life by preventing a feeling of connection to everyone and everything else. It's the depository of experience – but of a special type. It concerns those experiences that haven't been fully witnessed and resolved at the time; as a result, they continue to live on as a vibration in the Past time-body.

The Past time-body itself is made up of three layers, because there are different memory, or energetic, forms:

- **The Narrative past**: this is the story of the self, including your name, where you live, your culture and nationality.

- **The Knowledge past**: this is the problem-solving centre, which remembers how to build a shelf or fix a problem on a computer.

- **The Psychological past**: this is the storehouse of experiences that aren't fully witnessed, resolved or understood. Some psychologists call this the unconscious or the subconscious, but far from being unconscious, our Past is constantly seeking to be understood in a fully conscious moment and will create repeated patterns in order to do so.

The Potential centre

Why is it that we seem to create the life – and, indeed the world – that we focus on? Reality is a consensus view; you find that which you seek, you create that which you discover. This is possible only because you're also the Potential centre – the creative force and the potential field of all possibilities. One analogy is to see the Potential centre as the canvas, while the other two – the Present and the Past time-bodies – provide the paint and the brushwork. All three combine to make 'you', the artist.

In its passive state, the Potential centre is the silent witness to every experience, and it's this, and not the Past centre, that's the only true source of a sense of a continuous self, and one that's constant when we're awake and asleep.

The German philosopher Martin Heidegger said the greatest marvel was that there was life at all, when it was much more likely that there should be nothing. The miracle of life is made possible by the Potential centre. Through the filter of the Present time-body, this unified field expresses itself in space and time as separate and multiple representations of life.

While we live exclusively in – and through – the Present and Past time-bodies, we're blind to the unity of life; instead, we see its apparent diversity through the eyes of an individual who's separate from others. It's a phenomenon I call universal subjectivity – we all think we're having a separate experience although none of us actually is.

At the death of the body, the Present time-body dies too – and so, in that regard, neuroscience's view about your dying when your body does is correct. But the Past time-body lives on independently of the body for a period, and the length of that period is determined by the extent of the Past time-body's identification with the body. The Potential centre neither lives nor dies, as it's beyond both experiences.

Why is my story untrue?

Every one of us has our story. It's what we are, the character we carry around, and that responds to the world and acts in it. Our story places us in the world. As we've already seen, our story is made up of experiences – naturally enough – and many would argue that this all adds to the rich tapestry of life. Where would we be without our story? And isn't that which adds spice and drama to our lives, that makes it all worth living?

You pay a very high price to live by, and through, your untrue story. I suggest the price is too high. Anything from depression, addiction, anxiety and even suicide could be the price, and even if it's not that dramatic, it certainly is monotonous, tedious and joyless. The tedium is leavened by the occasional treat, such as a new car, a new pair of curtains and the occasional extramarital affair. It could also be the brake on your fulfilling yourself in the world, or expressing yourself fully.

So why is it untrue? At the mundane level, it can't be true because every experience is incomplete. It was your sense-impression of an event at the time, but if it was traumatic or extremely hurtful, it stays with you. It *is* you. It has to be untrue because every experience is from the perspective of your body at a particular point in time and space, and as most experiences involve somebody else, you've not witnessed the event in its completeness.

Others who may have witnessed an event were equally as partial. For example, if a parent tells a child that he or she wasn't good enough, it's a value judgement of that event and its outcome, and not of a person, but they make it so.

But there's something deeper and more wonderful about you that's drowned by the untrue story. It begins by identifying with the body – that one point in time and space – but you aren't a body, or not *just* a body. When you are born, you aren't immediately conscious that 'you' are a body; that happens only after there's pain and discomfort. We've already seen that there's an aspect of you – an impersonal self, admittedly – that's outside of time and space. If this aspect, which I call the Potential centre, becomes the most constant expression, you'll discover true joy and happiness. When time and space collapse, there's love.

Change and permanence

Using the model of the three time-bodies, the pivotal point of Buddhism and Taoism becomes clearer. Both philosophies tell us that the constant of life is suffering while we see ourselves as a permanent, fixed self. The world is always changing, and yet we either want things to stay as they are, or we build a wall of material things to protect us from the vicissitudes of life. However, we can't build certainty. At any moment we can lose our money, our home, our husband or wife.

We also have to understand exactly *what* is having this experience. If we see ourselves as a constant self, we'll suffer precisely because this idea is a fiction. Not only are we part of a life that's in flux, but we *are* that life itself. However, until we become conscious of the time-bodies, our sense of who we are changes, depending on the dominant pulse.

You might smell the scent of a flower one moment, then think of someone who upset you the next, then realize the beauty and wonder of the garden in which you find yourself. Each of those contrasting moods comes from one of the time-bodies, and the change can happen in moments.

The concept of a consistent self – the 'I' that records, interprets, and reacts – is described as the ego by some, who generally believe that the ego dies with the body, or as the soul by others, who imagine that this constant self survives death. While something does survive you, it's not the 'you' that you think it is! It's an impersonal self – but, then, there never was anything personal about life, not even 'your' life.

Applying the Time-Light model to the precepts of Buddhism, we see that the Present time-body's constant is change, while the Past time-body possesses an urge for repetition and a desire to have more of the same.

As we shall see, this urge from the Past time-body is a process in order to seek understanding and completion. Only when that's achieved will the pulses from the Past time-body diminish, and the patterns from the past disappear.

Why you're not present

You are the sum of one energy centre that creates time and space and a sense of self based on the body (the Present time-body); another that reinforces the sense of a separate self through the past (the Past time-body); and a third that's the creative field of all possibility, outside of time and space (the Potential centre).

While the Past time-body dominates, you're more the past than the present moment, and your experiences will tend to be a reiteration and a reliving of experience. You'll also have a keener sense of separation, even isolation, from the world and from others. You won't be completely 'there' attending in the present and so not be fully seeing and responding to the truth of the now.

Typical symptoms of a past-dominant life can be anything from aimless thinking or mental chatter, to mild depression, anxiety, a sense of worthlessness or a feeling that life is pointless. Its extreme expression is despair.

As your life is on constant repeat through the pulses of the Past time-body, you'll manifest patterns in your life – similar or even the same sort of things will tend to happen to you over and over – and you may have addictions. An addiction is not only a dependency on alcohol, drugs or gambling, but also repeated behavioural patterns that are possibly less damaging, or noticeable. They show up as a personality 'tic', a tendency always to do things the same way, or a common reaction to a person or the world that's similar, although the circumstance is different.

Everything is new in the now; if you lived entirely in the Present time-body you'd respond appropriately to each new experience as it arose, and you'd feel at one with it all. Even so, someone whose Present time-body is dominant wouldn't necessarily be aware of the Potential centre and the unity of all things.

Here are some examples of how the pulses may vary from person to person, or from time to time:

- **Small child**: Mainly Present, some Potential

- **Adolescent**: Mainly Present, some Past, a little Potential

- **Adult**: Some Present, mainly Past, a little Potential

- **Addict/Depressed person**: Mainly Past, little Present, almost no Potential

- **Saint/Realized person**: Mainly Potential, some Present, a little Past

Responding and reacting

As we age, we become more the past – the Psychological past in particular – which creates patterns from previous experiences that were not fully understood or resolved at the time, and that are lived out again in the present. Instead of responding, we react because the experience is familiar, and all the old emotions of fear, anger, or rejection well up again.

It's as if we're saying, 'I know what's happening here, I know what to expect from this person/situation.' In truth, we don't know what's going to happen because, in the present moment, everything is new and in flux. We only think we know because the situation has similarities to a previous experience.

A reaction invariably adds fuel to the flame, and the situation often escalates as a result. Let's take as an example a husband whose behaviour is constantly being challenged by his wife. This challenging creates an immediate pulse from the Psychological centre of the Past time-body that, almost instantaneously, is interpreted as a feeling or emotion, and then a series of thoughts. The reaction escalates the situation, whereas a response – the appropriate action in the present moment, and commensurate with the situation – would dissipate any energy around the exchange.

Suppose that, instead of *reacting* with: 'You're always trying to correct me. What about all your problems – let's look at those, shall we?' the husband was conscious enough – that is, conscious to the pulse from the past – to instead *respond* with: 'I see my behaviour is upsetting to you, as you're always pointing it out to me. What is it about it that so upsets you and how do you think I could do better?'

Few of us respond. Instead, we react to events in the present moment, which means that we're bringing the past to bear on the here and now. The present, which is rich with possibility, is constantly sabotaged by patterns from the past. As you get older, so the burden grows, and the patterns become denser. Eventually, you either become time-heavy, which quickens the death of the physical body, or you finally wake up to the pulse of feelings from the Past time-body.

If you do wake up, the past-to-present movement loses its power. You start to become time-light, and you live more in the present moment. You allow the pulses from the Present time-body to dominate, and you become more at one with the world and with everyone in it. The diminishing of the pulses from the Past time-body also allows the Potential centre to 'come through', and you, in the present moment, get a sense of unity, eternity and infinity. In that moment, you are natural, truly – and finally – a human being.

The diagram below shows the pulses that create a typical, 'healthy' you. The circles represent the three time-bodies and the smaller disc indicates where 'you' are at any one time.

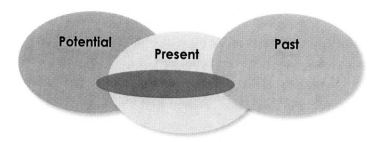

The pulses of the typical self

When we're children, we start out as time-light, and our untrue story has barely formed. We've had few experiences that we've not completely understood, and we live to an extent outside of time and space. We're in our own world – but the world 'out there' is also our home. Because the Potential centre is much more to the fore – its pulse is dominant – children actually are more outside of time and space than are most adolescents and adults.

Unless the child is abused – when pulses from the Present time-body and the Past centre start to dominate because the child is unable to fully comprehend what's happening to him – life seems to have an eternal glow, which we forever try to retrieve when we get older. Because we never seem to recreate those golden, timeless days of childhood, we compensate with cars, houses, career success and money, not realizing that these make us more time-heavy and take us even further away from the idyll of the Potential centre.

The pulses

All three energy centres communicate via pulses or waves, which are then interpreted into emotions and thoughts by the brain, especially by its ability to conceptualize. This gives substance to pulses that are derived from a painful or difficult experience, and they become expressions of fear, worry, doubt. The harnessing of the conceptual mind also begins to create patterns in the world that become your reality.

Most pulses derive from neutral experiences, which don't involve a feeling of hurt, fear or sadness, and these come from the Narrative and Knowledge past centres. That's how we make our way in the world and how we solve problems. However, the process becomes toxic when we create concepts from pulses from the Psychological past; past hurts and disappointments are given flesh by the conceptual mind, which defines them into a sense of a 'you' that's substantial, real and permanent. However, this sense of you separates you from the world, and the acid of past hurts dissolves the delicate thread that unites you to the field of all being.

The process of pulse-to-concept-to-substantial-you is a hopeless, reiterative loop, which is on constant repeat in the present in a vain attempt to be finally understood. It's hopeless because the past can never be recreated in the present; continuity and flux just don't mix. When pulses from the Narrative and Psychological time-bodies fuse, we can have war, terror and conflict, as national, racial or religious identity mix with a sense of past hurt and grievance.

> *While we're in thrall to pulses, we don't have true free will; instead, our bodies are commanded by the past and are no more conscious than a robot. Only someone who's free of his past is truly free, and who can claim to have free will. A conscious person – someone who's free from his past – is also freed from the karmic chain of cause and effect.*

Together, these three layers of the Past time-body go towards the creation of our sense of self. Without the Past centre, the Present would be pure consciousness – an observation of just what's in front of you at this moment. Is your father shouting at you right now? Of course not, all that's happening is a kettle boiling, or a bird singing in your garden, or music playing on the radio. Yet our father is still shouting at us through the psychological layer of our Past time-body.

Conversely, if we allow the pulses of the Potential centre to dominate, we have a rich sense of oneness and unity with everything around us. We're vessels that bring unity – or love – into a world that appears to be separate with multiple forms.

The diagram below shows the pulses of the enlightened self, which are similar to those of the newborn (see chapter 8). As before, the circles represent the three time-bodies and the smaller disc indicates where 'you' are at any one time.

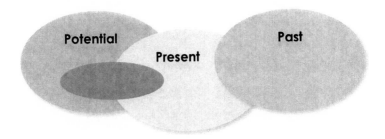

The pulses of the enlightened self

All of us walk around with a certain identity – I'm Jewish, or Christian, English or American – and these are memory forms from another part of the Past time-body, the Narrative centre. These truths and memory forms are usually harmless enough and become a possible threat to others and ourselves only if they're mixed with the hurts of the Psychological past.

The Knowledge past is the most important of the three layers of the Past time-body in terms of navigating your way around the world. You couldn't live a properly functioning life without it, as you wouldn't know anything about the world. You wouldn't know your name, where you lived, how to drive a car or what you'd learned.

The brain, the subconscious and the selves

Most neuroscientists hold to the theory that different areas of the brain are responsible for specific functions, such as memory or motor skills. However, some are beginning to understand the brain's complexity, and suggest that the hologram, where every part contains the whole, is a better model for understanding the brain's workings. New brain research supports this view.

Instead of seeing the brain as a hierarchy of sections, some neuroscientists are coming to the view that the brain's areas 'talk' to each other by way of circular loops in a distributed network, similar to the way that the internet is constructed.

The discovery, made by researchers from the US National Institutes of Health, suggests the brain doesn't have higher or lower centres of conscious thought, but works as a decentralized network. As a result, one area of the brain often compensates for another that may have been damaged.[1]

Even this explanation may not go far enough. If matter is viewed ultimately as energy that's palpable to the senses, then the brain becomes merely the receiving organ and interpreter of energy – and is itself a different expression of energy.

Some psychologists and therapists argue that phobias and trauma emanate from our subconscious or unconscious mind. However, I contend that they don't, because you don't have an unconscious or subconscious mind. It's a myth that we have come to accept through repeated telling, one to which some schools of psychology still cling.

Instead of a buried area of the mind that we don't have conscious access to, we have the Past centre and its three layers.

Within them, experiences reside as an energetic store. We may be unconscious of the movements from the Past centre, but that doesn't mean they reside in an actual 'unconscious'. On the contrary, everything seeks to become conscious, to reach an understanding, and to have an end in that knowing.

The drive to greater understanding is the one common theme of humanity throughout the ages. It's not only demonstrated in the sciences, but also in the arts, when the artist either seeks his or her own understanding or wants us to understand his or her vision.

Your past is no different; it's part of the energy flow towards understanding – yet it can reach its completion as a fully understood experience only in time and space, in the here and now. This moment is always the proving ground, the crucible in which an experience is either resolved or allowed to continue creating its patterns.

The woman who loved cakes

Joanna loved cakes. Indeed, she loved all the foods that were bad for her – and it showed. She was always fighting the flab, and rarely went down a dress size – except when she summoned up enormous willpower and went on a diet. She'd tried all the weight-loss programmes and the latest fads. They worked for a while, but she was always going back to the cakes, and so the pounds would go right back on again.

But what kept drawing her back to the 'bad foods', especially when she knew – in her rational brain, at least – that she'd put on more weight, and she'd hate herself for it?

She decided to find out, and she visited a local hypnotist who was known for her ability to help people with weight issues. Joanna doubted that she'd be able to 'go under', but she did – although the experience was not as she'd expected. She was conscious, and she 'knew' she was being hypnotized, and yet she couldn't help herself. When the hypnotist told her that her eyelids were getting heavy, they started to fall. When the hypnotist told her to raise her right arm, she did, even though she tried to fight it.

After a few simple exercises, the hypnotist invited Joanna to go back to her earliest memories, especially any that were associated with food. Almost immediately, Joanna saw herself as a five-year-old, sitting in the kitchen of her grandparents' home. The grandparents were arguing; the grandmother was accusing her husband of having a girlfriend. Joanna was waiting to have a meal with them, but the grandmother was letting the food burn on the stove. From there, other memories of food and emotional issues – ones that she'd 'forgotten' – started to arise.

Hypnotism is a good technique for accessing the oldest memories from the Psychological past, allowing them to rise up without any interpretation or justification from the conceptual mind. It allows you to see the memory clearly, the pulse of the trapped emotion, the experience you can't understand. In Joanna's case, she was just a five-year-old in the centre of an emotional crisis in the family.

Finally, at the age of 43, Joanna was able to see the whole situation – the little girl that she then was, the emotional turmoil of her grandparents – and forgive them and herself. As soon as she did that, the desire for cakes vanished in the forgiveness that crossed time and space.

All desires are equal

Some of us who realize that money in the bank won't scratch the metaphysical itch of feeling hollow and unfulfilled instead turn to religion and spirituality. However, until we wake up to the past-to-present movement, we're in danger of merely adding to the weight of the past.

There's no qualitative difference between wanting to be a millionaire and wanting spiritual fulfilment or enlightenment. Both are different expressions of the same energy flow, and both will make you more time-heavy. I call this phenomenon the 'hungry mind' – we've all experienced this craving for another book, or a new car, or a better home, convinced that this very latest acquisition will be all we need to make us happy, to provide the key to fulfilment or any other ambition we've set ourselves in time.

This idea – that a desire for enlightenment and a desire to be a millionaire are not qualitatively different – may seem shocking to you; if it is it's probably because you have a value system that rates the pursuit of money as bad, and the pursuit of God as good, without seeing that the pursuit in and of itself is the problem. Any pursuit involves a 'you' at a certain point in space and time who seeks something else imagined as better, which is a projection from the Past time-body.

You can get a good idea of a person's current state by that which he or she imagines as the state of enlightenment: if a person views it as a state of constant happiness, the person is unhappy; if another sees it as a state of peace, then that person is in turmoil.

The future holds nothing better than what you have right now. In fact, the idea of the future is merely a mental projection. There's nothing you can add to your life that would make you more complete than you already are; on the contrary, it's purely the pursuit of that 'better' state that's making you unhappy.

Seeing that on its own is not enough. The Past time-body will continue to pulse through to the Present centre as long as it has unfinished business. You can't re-enact previous experiences in order finally to understand them, as the circumstances will have changed and the players in the original drama may even be dead.

However, you can become conscious of those vibrations of experience through forgiveness and understanding. Both skills require seeing the situation in its totality – the people involved and the circumstance in which they all found themselves. This might seem to be an impossible feat, but it can happen at a point of great stillness, when the three time-bodies coordinate. I shall be showing you how to do that in the Time-Light programme.

Summary

It's one of mankind's greatest fictions that you are an autonomous, independent and free individual who can control your emotions, passions and thoughts. Only when the processes of thought are clearly observed can you see that you're the creation of the emotions, passions and thoughts.

Chapter 8
Your Present Time-Body

'Man has no Body distinct from his Soul for that call'd Body is a portion of Soul discern'd by the five Senses, the chief inlets of Soul in this age.'

William Blake

Where's the focus of your attention right now? Hopefully, it's on the pages of this book. That's pretty much how we operate most of the time: our focus is invariably a metre (3 ft) or so in front of us, and this is the natural 'resting' place of consciousness. We become aware of our body only when there's discomfort or pain, or when we feel hungry or tired.

This sense of being, with the focus around us, is how we are when we're born. The untrue story of you begins with the identification with a body, which becomes you. Before your body was conceived, you were purely Potential, a unified field, or unknowing consciousness outside of time and space.

On the death of your body, you'll be that centre again. The Present time-body grows as the body forms in the womb and finally comes into the world with the body's birth. By this time, the Present time-body is complete, and creates and supports the world in space and time.

Although the sense of separation, division, and multiplicity seems like the only reality, it's but one of three realities that make you 'you'. The ultimate truth remains that you're an undivided field, which supports all life and is all life. That's your true home when time and space collapse with the death of the body.

The final twist is that the 'you' that's a unified field is not that which you may believe yourself to be. It's an impersonal you that also shines out from the eyes of everyone around you. It's the unified field made separate and individual, a multiple expression of unity. The fact that your parents were already experiencing the world as time and space before you were born suggests that they and you, as bodies and brains, are part of this impersonal field.

When you were time-light

In the first few months of life, when you were living largely from the Potential and Present centres, you were extremely time-light. The Past time-body hasn't properly formed since the newborn has had few experiences that haven't been fully witnessed or understood, other than the trauma of birth. That first experience leaves an energy pattern forming the skeleton that will allow the Past time-body to develop. Experiences that are neutral or don't engage the entity of past sadness or hurts don't leave an imprint in the Past time-body.

Child-development experts say that in the first few days and weeks of its life, a newborn is unable to differentiate between itself and a world outside. While the child lives in the Potential centre, there's no division. Philosophers say something similar: a baby and indeed a very young child can't comprehend that there are 'other minds' in the world besides its own.

For the newborn, the pulses primarily come from the Potential and Present time-bodies, as there is little or no past self, as the diagram below shows.

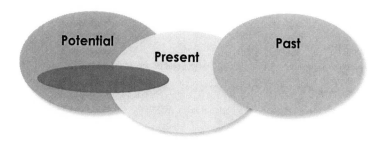

The pulses of the newborn

The Present becomes the dominant pulse only when the baby has a physical need, and the first schism arises when the world doesn't satisfy it – when the mother is unable to feed the child or its cries go unanswered. This creates an energy print of upset or concern: it's a new pattern for the baby, and it becomes an early expression of the Past centre. An energetic entity of sadness is being formed.

Apart from the primitive energy pattern created with the trauma of birth, fear and a lack of satisfaction are invariably some of the first experiences that the Present centre is unable to understand fully. This incomplete experience – seen from your own limited and body-centred perspective – begins to form in the Past time-body.

The origins of the Past time-body are therefore pain, fear, and hurt; the child becomes the adult who spends the rest of his life running from those earliest and primitive emotions in search of pleasure and gratification. From these feelings the child also has the first intimations that it may be different, and separate, from the world.

The Present time-body has a memory, but it's simple in comparison to that of the Past. Its needs and desires primarily consist of food, shelter, warmth, and other bodily needs, including sex, and so any emotion associated with these leaves its own energy imprint. They usually revolve around sensations of fear and pleasure: one is to be avoided, the other to be pursued.

Simple memories such as these have reverberations in the Past time-body. As we shall see in the next chapter, most events that are not neutral are extended, shaped, and given a meaning in the Past time-body until the energetic imprint of the experience becomes a model of reality. One bad experience of X is extended in time until we have our model that tells us something about the world out there: that all Xs are always bad.

Most of us generalize from a bad experience to some greater or lesser extent. This tendency is the bedrock of prejudice. One day you're mugged by a shaven-headed youth in Detroit, and from that you create a model of reality that all shaven-headed youths are violent, or that Detroit's a violent city. If you get food poisoning after eating a meal at a local restaurant, your model of the world tells you that the restaurant is to be avoided because it serves poisonous food.

Models of reality aren't always wrong – they're based on sense data, after all, even though it may be partial or incomplete. These models are, however, invariably not true, because they're a description, a past impression imposed on the changing present moment.

If we were able to live entirely in the Present, we'd see every experience as new and different, which of course it is. As such, we'd respond to a situation – the appropriate method of meeting any experience – instead of reacting to it, which we do when we live from the Psychological past.

The drive of all Three Selves is towards greater understanding. For the Present, this is mainly achieved through the sciences as it attempts to explain the world and the universe. Nevertheless, the sciences explain only the Present centre, the world of phenomena, which can be named, categorized and measured, or theoretically demonstrated through mathematics.

As the sciences are derived from the same time-and-space continuum that they explore, scientists often fail to see their limitation, as they and their tools are part of that which they measure and analyze.

As there's no apparent evidence of God in the Present, the sciences tend towards the view that there's no God. But that's only one-third of the story. God as a first causal agent – the first observer, if you like – would be outside of the time and space that it's created, and so scientists within time and space wouldn't have the capability to know God.

The world as facts

In reality, in the here and now, there are no problems. There are only facts. It's a fact there's a war; it's a fact that children are starving in Africa. As such, the Present responds to a situation; it's the appropriate method of meeting any experience.

You'll discover in the Time-Light programme that there are only two things you can do with a fact: either you act on it or you're unable to do anything because it's outside of your powers to do so. A problem, on the other hand, is a loop system that has no resolution, and instead creates a pattern of worry, as happens with the constant iteration of the pulses from the Psychological past. It's also the beginnings of depression, as the rational mind seeks to find an answer – and can't.

The conceptual brain

The Present time-body also includes the brain, with all its neural firings and its hemispheric interplays. The main modus operandi of the brain's thought processes is the use of concepts, a remarkable intellectual leap that appears to separate us from all the other animals of the Earth in terms of complexity. With a conceptual mind, we conjure up dimensional models that allow us to build a world of houses, temples, roads, bridges, vehicles, ships, planes and space rockets.

However, the conceptual mind is a false friend. Although it allows us to build a world, it also separates us from a direct experience of being. The word 'flower', for example, stands in the way of the thing itself. We satisfy ourselves by living second-hand lives at one remove from being, and we're content to experience life through words, symbols, images, and equations. We've become so hypnotized by them that we study the finger that points at the moon and no longer see the moon itself. While we're satisfied with a name for a description of the strangeness of things, we live a superficial life.

The conceptual brain separates things into discrete bundles, and we see this demonstrated in virtually every human activity, from the sciences and medicine to technology to education. The reality is otherwise: things are indescribable and they're part of a whole.

Concepts also make tangible any feelings that are inchoate or have an undefined reverberation. Almost every thought and emotion you have is reliant on a concept, including the endless internal monologue and chatter that accompanies almost every waking moment, as well as your assumptions, your beliefs – your entire frame of reference about the world 'out there'.

The actualizing machine

Such is the power of the Present time-body when it joins with the creative energies of the Past and the Potential centres that the combination becomes an actualizing machine. Every thought that you think is true about yourself eventually appears in the world. If you convinced yourself – no doubt through criticism from others – that you're poor at mathematics, you'll demonstrate that 'truth' about yourself in the world by failing at mathematics. If parents aren't up to the task, schools are excellent places where these feelings of lack, which last a lifetime, begin.

The philosopher Sam Keen once gave a good example of the processes of the actualizing machine. Throughout his formative years, his parents told him he was useless at mechanical things. He couldn't fix anything, his parents regularly reminded him, and of course so it proved to be. However, as an adult, he took a test with all the usual pressures removed – and he recorded one of the highest possible scores for mechanical ability. His innate skills made him a mechanical genius, but the actualizing machine of the brain had put him at the bottom of the class.

The world is made real by our imprinting of time and space, and the internal monologue and our emotional responses are made tangible by the conceptual mind. By definition, every concept is but a representation, and yet it's often more real to us than even the ground we walk on, so close is our internal world to us.

> *Our concepts run deep; it's a concept that there's time and space, it's a concept that there's a world that's separate and 'out there'. The idea that your happiness will be found in that world is a concept; even the idea that you have a body is a concept!*

Of course, the belief that 'you' are a body is a pivotal concept because everything else rests on it, from your own sense of identity to your place in the world and your relationship to it. A concept may be a useful form of shorthand that allows you to navigate in the world, but in so doing you've replaced reality – the immediate experience – with the conceptual description.

One of the principal tenets of Buddhism is that we must rid ourselves of the conceptual mind, so let's see how Buddhism would disabuse us of the concept that we have a body. In endeavouring to demonstrate that you have one, you might first point to some vague area around your chest or point at your head. No, says our Buddhist, that's your chest or your head. Where's your body?

So you do a giant circle that encompasses everything: the head, the feet, the arms, the chest, and so on. Therefore, says the Buddhist, you're telling me the body is everything; let me make a list. So he proceeds to do so as if he were an auditor marking off the assets at the year-end. That's eight fingers, two thumbs, two arms, two eyes, two ears, one head, two knees, and so on. The body equals (which means it's the exact same as) all these individual items.

Three months later you phone the Buddhist auditor with the sad news that you've had an accident. In an unfortunate grass-cutting incident, you've lost a finger. The Buddhist sympathizes and tells you you've lost more than a finger – you've lost your whole body. How can that be, you ask? Because eight fingers were part of the sum total of all the parts that exactly equated to 'the body', he says, and now that you have seven, the whole sum collapses. This sounds like a clever party trick, but it also happens to be true. The body is nothing more than a concept – a descriptive shorthand that makes everyday life possible.

Summary

The natural 'resting' place of consciousness is around a metre (3 ft) in front of you. This is consciousness in the present moment, but it's difficult to sustain that if we need to act in the world. For that we need concepts and memory, but these become the dominant forces that define us, as we'll see in the next chapter.

Chapter 9
Your Past Time–Body

'The degree of one's emotions varies inversely with one's knowledge of the facts.'

BERTRAND RUSSELL

Why do you think? Why do emotions suddenly well up? Moreover, what in you creates the constant thoughts – the 'chattering monkey', as some Eastern religions call it – that accompanies your almost every waking moment and often your dreams? These thoughts are not problem-solving; they're the inconsequential mental mutterings that take on enormous significance, giving substance to this sense of 'me'.

Because we're doing it all the time, and we're often unaware of the process, it's not apparent how it happens, or indeed why. If you were to observe the phenomenon, you'd see that it's a movement of time – from the past to the present, often to some imagined future.

Without the past, you wouldn't have the narrator, the constant chattering companion for every experience. The narrator's nourishment is past experience, and it's the brain in the Present self that latches onto the energetic pulses from the past and turns them into thoughts or a feeling.

Every thought begins as a pulse from the Past self,
but it happens instantaneously, and it's almost
impossible to see this happening. However, once it's
begun, it becomes a symbiotic dance between the
present and the past. Thoughts from the present
then create more pulses from the past, back and
forth, in a flow that seems to be endless.

As the dance continues through the years, so the sense of a substantial 'you' builds and separates you from the world and from others. It's a dead-end. Eventually, we feel completely isolated and cut off from the world. This anguish is the beginning of depression, anxiety and a sense of despair and pointlessness, and the starting point for addictive behaviour. It's astonishing to realize that the two greatest psychological or spiritual crises of modern times – depression and addiction – have the exact same roots.

The energetic layers of the Past time-body

Some basic emotions arise from the Present time-body, but most begin as a pulse from the Past time-body, and the conceptual brain gives them substance. If concepts didn't immediately arise, there would be just the pulse, which would dissipate without the fuel injection of concepts and emotions.

The Present time-body has its own emotions, such as anger, fear, and disgust, but these are immediate responses to something in the moment. Once the danger or object of disgust has passed, so too does the accompanying emotion. It's only if you're not fully conscious in that moment that the emotion will form an energy print in the Past and eventually regenerate.

Experiences have different granulations. You couldn't compare an event such as going to your favourite coffee shop or fixing a chair with the death of your spouse and conclude that they were similar. They form different memories, and they're captured in one of the Past time-body's three energetic layers:

The Knowledge past

This is where the conceptual brain in the Present time-body and the Past work together in order to solve a problem, such as how to mend a fuse, understand a situation in the Present, or remember where someone lives or where you parked your car.

The Narrative past

These pulses, the ones that invariably create the 'chattering monkey', tell you who you are in the world: the picture you build of your spouse, your cultural heritage, your position in the world. The Narrative is the Past time-body that also fuels inconsequential thoughts or a melody you can't get out of your head.

It gives you your sense of identity, a personality trait, or a series of beliefs from your upbringing and culture that tell you that you're a Christian, a Muslim, or an atheist. Although its chatter is relatively harmless, it nevertheless provides a filter across the Present centre that prevents it from having a direct experience of the here and now.

The Narrative is not so harmless when it fuses with the hurts of the Psychological past. This mix is the origin of war, violence or terrorism. Our beliefs about religion or nationality become toxic when we add the chemicals of hurts, a sense of injustice or right. War and suffering occur because we're unconscious to these drives from the Past. History, hurts and division, as concepts from the Past, take on a greater significance than the here and now, and allow us to kill another human being standing in front of us.

The Psychological past

This layer is made up of experiences we've not fully understood, from unresolved conflict, hurts, fears, and trauma, to moments of joy and ecstasy. It exists because we've not fully witnessed an experience – we've failed to fully understand or observe. We can't understand an experience if we've been the central player and it's been seen entirely through our eyes, standpoint or needs.

Furthermore, we've experienced it at a fixed point in space and time, without being aware of the causal chain that led to it. When an experience isn't fully witnessed, an energy print of hurt or fear is left in the Psychological past, and it'll replay the event in the Present time-body – your day-to-day reality – in order to reach resolution and completion. It's a hopeless endeavour, however.

As any action takes place only in the Present time-body, the people and the circumstances will inevitably have changed, as these are from a past that no longer exists. Receiving the pulses from the Psychological past, the brain's conceptual abilities can do only one of three things.

It either begins creating a pattern in the world that's as close to the original situation as possible, or it creates a displacement, as I call it, where the feeling is similar – such as a sense of loss – but the player or circumstance is different. For example, if a sense of loss for a dead parent is projected onto someone living, the emotional response when that person goes away for any reason is disproportionate to the event.

The third possibility is the creation of a mirror pattern, which is a reaction to an experience that's its complete opposite, such as an overwhelming desire for wealth based on a pulse from an earlier experience or fear of poverty. While there's nothing 'wrong' in wanting to improve yourself and your lot, or in wishing for a better start for your children, a mirror pattern is all-consuming and can even be life-threatening, as happened to Charles Dickens (see chapter 2).

The woman who blew up the world

The past not only shapes our reality, it also shapes the world. Hanifah is a special Arabic name for a girl. It means 'true believer', and it's a great honour and responsibility for all girls who are so named. Several years ago, a US Newsweek journalist interviewed a Palestinian woman called Hanifah. Beautiful and intelligent, she'd graduated with a degree in law five years before, and now she was the mother of a darling daughter, aged one. Hanifah had recently celebrated her 28th birthday when she spoke on the eve of the 'greatest day of my life', as she described it.

The following day she left her neighbourhood in Palestine, passed through the heavily guarded border crossing into Israel, where she stopped for a moment, smiling at the young guard who seemed to like her, before heading to the school gymnasium, where she worked as a teacher's aid. Although she was an Arab who prayed to Allah, Hanifah was liked and trusted by the staff and the children, and their friendship seemed to transcend the obvious differences of race, culture, and religion.

This special relationship had alerted the terrorist cell to which Hanifah's younger brother belonged. They approached her and asked if she was prepared to be a martyr, and kill the persecutors of her people. Without hesitation, she agreed.

So, on that very special day, after heading to the gymnasium, Hanifah detonated the bombs strapped around her body. She killed three children, and maimed five others in what was described as yet another terrorist outrage in the Middle East.

'I want people to ask: "Why? Why should a beautiful young girl, with everything to live for, who had a lovely baby daughter, why should she kill herself and the children in her care?" she'd told the journalist. 'I want them to investigate, and find out how we live in Palestine, being bombed every day, losing our family, our children, our homes.'

Hanifah's act of 'terrorism' triggered a wave of missiles onto the poor homes of Palestine from Israeli encampments close to the border, an attack that was described on the news in the West that evening as 'justified reprisals'.

For Hanifah, the hurts that pulsed from her Psychological past fused with the pulses from her Narrative past to create a volatile mix. It's not unique; we all do this to some extent. Our thoughts loom over us in the present moment, and seem more real and substantial than the pavement beneath our feet. Our thoughts shape us. Our thoughts make a hell out of a heaven, and these thoughts — from experiences — make us ill. They can even kill us.

Beliefs shape the nation-state. Beliefs, as a group thought, set nation against nation.

Experiences that aren't fully witnessed

What's an experience that hasn't been fully witnessed? It's one in which only 'you' appear. You also fail to see the true nature of the other persons – and their true nature is as a Three-Selves being.

A partially experienced event involves just you when, in fact, there are at least two players, plus the context of the circumstances surrounding the experience. You can't fully understand anything if you see it only from your own perspective, which is held by a wounded, self-protective entity incapable of truly understanding any event.

Even a tragic and untimely death isn't understood until we fully realize who we are. When we do, we see that we are three time-bodies, and only one – the Present time-body – can physically die. It's still cause for grief and sadness when it happens, of course, but death is not the whole story.

You also bring your assumptions, prejudices, and beliefs to every situation, and these, too, are the creation of partially seen and understood previous experiences. In essence, you've failed to gain sufficient altitude over a situation, and as a result, it's not been fully witnessed.

In my own case (you can read my full story in chapter 1), I had a miserable childhood because of the wretched way my father behaved towards me. He wouldn't acknowledge me and for the first seven years of my life only whistled at me when he wanted my attention. I couldn't understand this bizarre behaviour and, of course, it left an emotional scar.

Without the support and approval of my father, I was unable properly to function in the world as a young adult. I couldn't apply for promotion to a new position, for example, because I didn't think I'd be good enough. I couldn't even bring myself to go into a clothes shop to buy a new shirt because I didn't think I deserved one.

It started to make sense only when I was an adult, on one afternoon when my parents revealed something very private about their marriage. In that moment, all sorts of experiences I'd had as a child started to make sense. I saw events outside of my own perspective. It wasn't about me. It never was.

Everything fell into place: I knew then – and completely – why my father behaved in the way he did. Yes, it was infantile and petty, but it was understandable. The understanding was a salve; but more than that, the weight was lifted.

This realization was the beginning, not the end. I still needed my partner, Lynne, to point out when I was being unconscious to the movements from the Past time-body, and this continued to happen occasionally, until I could see the pattern for myself. It worked both ways: I was able to help Lynne see patterns in her life, too.

That, for me, is the essence of a wonderful relationship: where either partner helps the other to become conscious. Most people marry and believe that's the end point, that life is already complete. Marriage and partnerships provide situations for growing and becoming conscious. As most people don't see that, they end up rowing and, eventually, divorcing from a sense of bitter disappointment or resentment.

Neutral and ecstatic experiences and addiction

Not all experience results in a feeling of sadness, hurt, or resentment. Much of it is neutral, but sometimes the experience is ecstatic, an oceanic feeling of unity or great joy. We don't understand these heightened experiences any more than we know why we feel sad or hurt. We don't know that they're the pulses from the Potential centre.

However, once the feeling passes, the basic movement of the pulses from the Psychological past to the Present time-body is the same: we want to repeat the experience in order to understand it. The difference with an ecstatic feeling is that we endeavour to engineer the recurrence of the feeling by replicating, as closely as possible, the circumstances that led to the oceanic uprush.

This is the seed of addictive behaviour. Whatever was happening at the time of the joyful surge of feeling – whether it was sex, drink or driving a fast sports car, perhaps – may become the subject of the addiction; we strive to have the experience again and so we repeat the activity that we associate with the feeling, because we want to understand – to know where it came from.

In one or more areas of our lives, most of us lie somewhere along the spectrum of addictive behaviour. We may engage in a habitual pattern, a mild addiction, or a pattern so destructive that it wrecks our life and that of others. We're addicted because of the pulses, on constant replay, that come from the Past time-body.

The sudden feeling of joy, completeness, or unity is our natural state, and it emanates from the Potential centre. It can happen suddenly and without our seeking it; in fact, it's most likely to happen when the Past time-body is quiet. When it does we often make a wrong association between the feeling and whatever we're doing at the time – we believe there's a direct cause-effect between what we're doing and the sudden sense of joy.

This feeling of unity and completeness could happen, for example, while we're drinking a glass of wine. Because we don't understand the process or know of the existence of the Potential centre, we somehow associate the feeling with the wine. This is an example of associated addiction, in which the sense of joy and completeness occurs unbidden and as if by accident while doing something else.

A direct addiction is experienced by drug addicts, for example, who are seeking out this feeling consciously through the use of cocaine, heroin or LSD. The drug addict ends their addiction only when they learn how to get in touch with the feeling of unity, love, and completeness naturally. The body also has a chemical addiction, and we look at this in more detail in the Time-Light programme.

> *No matter its source, the feeling – and the desire to*
> *repeat the feeling – is the beginning of addiction.*
> *In a process that I call psychological witchcraft, the*
> *person with the associated addiction in particular*
> *replicates as best he can the circumstances from the*
> *original sensation in the hope of repeating it.*

As we've seen, the sense of unity actually happened because the Past time-body was quiet, thus allowing the pulses from the Potential centre to dominate. However, these pulses are submerged by those from the Past time-body, as it seeks to repeat the experience.

Ironically, the more we want to replicate the experience, the more the pulses from the Past obscure the oceanic feeling from the Potential centre. As a result, we try a little harder to have that experience again, so we take another glass of wine and then another, or we desire more sex, depending on the circumstances when the oceanic feeling occurred. Before long, we've become addicts.

Addiction and depression can have several origins: one can be purely chemical, and witnessed in the Present time-body, and another can be a sense of hopelessness, as the iterative pulses from the Past time-body seek a resolution, but can't find one. Addiction and depression can indeed have their origins in sadness and despair, as most psychologists would recognize, but paradoxically they can also derive from a fleeting sense of great joy and completeness.

As such, these feelings are intelligent because they seek complete understanding. An alcoholic doesn't always drink because he's unhappy; he may drink because he wants to be happy and whole again. Essentially, an addict *feels* more acutely.

Understanding addiction in this way is the starting point to ending it. An addiction doesn't need to be suppressed or denied; it's an impulse that's trying to become conscious and understood. This is the beginning of intelligence and the end of addiction, a process that can be completed when you carry out the exercises in the Time-Light programme.

The past in the present

Whereas addictive behaviour can be an active attempt to recreate the ecstatic moment, most movements from the Past time-body happen because something in life creates the circumstances that cause the past hurts to resurface. Of course, that 'something', the event, is initiated by the actualizing brain via the pulses from the Past, but we're unconscious of that movement. It may be something that someone says or does, or a situation that we witness.

This happens to all of us from time to time – when our buttons get pushed, and the energetic entity is activated. It is, as we've seen, the Past trying to re-experience itself. It's a moment of recognition as the Past imprints itself on the Present.

Invariably, the result is a reaction in the Present – a blind and involuntary response to a situation or experience. It's as though the brain is saying, 'I know what's going to happen here.' In a sense, it does. Although every experience in the Present is new and different, the pulses from the Past ensure that patterns are re-established, and so a previous experience is re-experienced in the Present.

It could be likened to the points on a train track shifting and the train – your sense of a permanent self – being forced along a track that it's been down before instead of continuing a journey into new and uncharted territory. This pattern is on constant repeat, and it'll come to the fore at any opportunity when an experience in the Present seems similar to an unresolved issue that exists as an energy imprint in your Psychological past.

The extension of experiences in time

The Psychological past centre 'knows' the other two energy centres – it's aware of them both. The Present is a necessary expression of the Potential centre in space and time, but its own needs are modest, if not basic, and it merely desires a sufficiency for its survival. It knows nothing of the Potential self.

The Past reflects both the glory of the Potential centre and the primitive of the Present, and from that it creates the sorrow and tensions of life. If we allow the Past centre to dominate – and we do so by being unaware of its pulses that are translated by the brain – we never feel complete, never believe we have enough.

The Past will extend in time the simple needs and pleasures of the Present. The Present needs shelter: the Past desires a castle. The Present needs food: the Past yearns for a feast. The Present needs sex: the Past lusts after pornography.

The Present may have experiences – pleasurable and fearful – that are also extended in time. Experiences in the Present cause sensations of pleasure, pain, or indifference – the latter happen with neutral experiences. Although these experiences are isolated, they're given substance in the Psychological past until they start to form our models of reality, so that one event becomes a truth that's so in every circumstance, every time. We do this constantly while we're unconscious of the process. It's the birthplace of prejudice, opinions, and world views. A simple fear becomes morbid.

The Past is always an extension through time of our basic needs, driving the complex desires, fears and pleasures of the Present. In so doing, the Past creates Psychological time, an energetic movement from a past and into a projected future. That movement alone creates the imagined future, a fictitious place.

And there will always be that ache – that lack of something more that we just can't define. Most of us seek it in material rewards, but all the time, we somehow know the satisfaction won't last. We might look for it in sexual adventures, or in drink, or drugs or gambling, yet we know that we'll crash down from the high or quickly tire of any new sexual thrill.

Ultimately, a few of us look to fill that ache through religion and spirituality – but all the time it's the Past centre striving for the very thing it can't have. The only way 'you' can get rid of the ache is to stop the process that is the ache itself – the Psychological past, ever seeking to complete experiences it never understood. Only when that stops does the Potential centre become dominant. That's the first and last freedom, the only freedom.

The birth of depression

Although all of us are influenced by the past, some of us are overwhelmed by the Past time-body. When this happens, the world gets too much for us. We lose sight of any worthwhile purpose to our life. Nothing pleases us, and nothing delights us. We also feel alienation – from the world, from others and even from our own body.

These are all symptoms of mild depression. It happens because we've become time-heavy. We have too much past, and it becomes the filter through which we see the world. As a result, we lose any perspective because we no longer have direct experience of the world around us. Instead, we see the past; worse, we're the past incarnate.

You could be walking through a beautiful park, but you're not present – you're thinking about your business problems. You could be playing with your child, but you're only going through the physical motions – you're worried about tomorrow's appointment with the doctor.

Some cases of depression and addiction are the result of an ecstatic experience. The depressed person or addict finds life after the experience to be mundane and wants to have it again. As the illustration below shows, the ecstatic experience is an unacknowledged cause of depression and addiction. The other is trauma that wasn't fully witnessed in that moment; that is, it was viewed, at best, only from the perspective of the body-centred self.

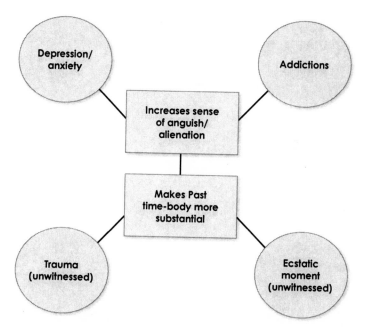

The common origins of depression and addiction

While the movement of the past happens to all of us some of the time, it becomes the entire life of the depressed person. The chatter from the Past time-body has become constant and even accompanies the person in his sleep. By this point, the person is haunted, and the Present has become shadowy. The Potential has all but disappeared.

Why has this happened? We've already seen that the Past time-body is seeking full understanding of experiences, and it does this in the only way it can – as pulses to the Present time-body. The Present is the only one of the Three Selves where experience happens, because it's the only one in time and space. The Past seeks to have experience re-enacted in order finally to complete the experience.

The pulses from the Past time-body therefore seek an experiential solution, and not an intellectual one. You can't think or rationalize the completion of an experience – you must *feel* it – and totally. Understanding can't be achieved through the intellect, paradoxical as that may initially sound.

For example, you could intellectually grasp that your mother always told you that you weren't good enough, but that doesn't make the hurt go away. You have to become conscious of those feelings in the Present in order to reach full and final understanding – and ultimately forgiveness.

The depressed person is endeavouring to achieve just that – a rational resolution to an irrational problem. Eventually, the Past becomes an obsession as he tries to resolve problem after problem arising from the Past time-body. Yet the pulses from the Past are not 'problems' per se, but incomplete experiences It's a tragic and hopeless exercise. The Past is just that; it can't be recreated. People and the original circumstances have changed. So, the Present does the best it can, creating a close associative approximation and thus a pattern in your life, or a mirror reaction or displaced concept, where an unrelated person or situation becomes the subject of a previous experience.

The chronically depressed person is almost entirely dominated by pulses emanating from the Past centre, and the Psychological past in particular – as seen in the diagram below. Overwhelmed by these pulses, he or she is often unaware of the present moment and its beauty.

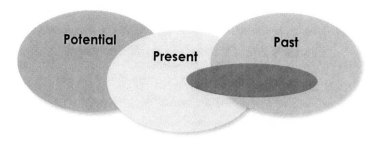

The pulses of the chronically depressed self

The man who repeated himself

Bessel van der Kolk, a psychiatrist, originally handled the following case. Peter Levine later related it in his book Waking the Tiger *(North Atlantic Books, 1997).*

On one 5 July in the late 1980s, a man walked into a convenience store at 6:30 in the morning. He held his finger in his pocket in such a way as to simulate a gun. As the store had only just opened, the cashier had just a few dollars in loose change to hand over. Satisfied with his haul, the gunman left the store, and sat in his car until the police arrived. When they did, he got out of his car and with his finger in his pocket, said that he had a gun and that everyone should stay away.

The police soon realized that the 'gun' was a finger, and the man was arrested. At the police station, the officer in charge discovered that identical crimes had occurred on six previous occasions over the past 15 years, each happening at 6:30 a.m. on 5 July.

The man said that he was a Vietnam veteran, and the police realized that there was more to the crime than the usual hold-up. They took him to the nearby veterans' hospital to meet the resident psychiatrist, Dr Bessel van der Kolk.

The veteran told van der Kolk his story. When he was in Vietnam, the Viet Cong ambushed his platoon. Everyone other than him and his friend, Jim, had been killed. This tragic event happened on 4 July. As night fell, the rescue helicopters were unable to find the pair, and so they spent a terrifying night, surrounded by the Viet Cong. At approximately 3:30 a.m. Jim was picked off by a sniper and shot in the chest. He died three hours later – in the arms of the veteran – at 6:30 a.m. on 5 July.

On his return to the USA, the veteran re-enacted the anniversary of his friend's death by holding staged hold-ups. As he explained, he didn't do it every year, because he was in jail the years that he missed. By staging the robberies, the veteran was recreating the fire fight, which escalated, just as it had in the past, whenever the police arrived. In the wrong hands, the veteran might have been dismissed as mad, but fortunately, van der Kolk was able to help him see that he was acting out the past in order to resolve a deep emotional scar.

Using the Three Selves model, we see that the pulses from the Psychological past were being interpreted and re-enacted in the Present. The veteran was attempting to replicate the original situation in order to resolve it.

Your untrue story

We've looked at the influence of unresolved experiences that reside as energetic imprints in the Psychological past, but what of the other two centres in the Past self? One's own story, as stored in the Narrative centre, doesn't always lead us to war and conflict; it also provides the backdrop for our identity in the world. While it may be true that I'm white and Anglo-Saxon, brought up in a democratic, Christian country, these truths are relatively so and have meaning only because others are not Christian, white and Anglo-Saxon.

These facts about me – my story – are given depth, colour and shading by my experiences until they become the truth by which I live and determine who 'I' am. Through experience, my story creates a value system that determines the things with which I wish to identify, and those I don't. Once established, my story then presents itself to the world in what we might call a personality, although it's certainly not a consistent self. No personality remains the same all the time, because there are always various forces at play.

Nevertheless, there's a persistency of type made up by characteristics that developed with our earliest experiences but have been either amplified or suppressed by experience, culture and upbringing. That's why we sometimes do something 'out of character' – a wonderful expression that illustrates the play-acting nature of our story – and suddenly lose our temper or become moody or violent.

The constant chatter, the non-stop monologue that accompanies our every step, also adds potency to a sense of self by way of the Narrative time-body. Almost from the moment we wake up and until we sleep – and often while we sleep – our narrative, our personal backstory, keeps up an inconsequential commentary of everything that's happening around us.

You in the world

Another layer of the Past also helps to create the sense of 'you'. The Knowledge past is the storehouse for everything you know or have learned about yourself and the world. Personal knowledge adds colour to the 'you' – because of it, you know where you live, whether you're married and have children, where you work, and what you do there.

It also stores impersonal knowledge, which helps us function in the world, although generally this type of information is less important than personal knowledge. It's more important that I know where my home is, for instance, than whether I can point to Kenya on a map. Nevertheless, together they help fuel the narrative, your story.

And so it is that the three layers of the Past time-body flow back and forth with the Present and its conceptual brain, creating the sense of a solid, never-changing and continuous self. Increasingly, this sense of self develops more time and space between it and the world.

Summary

Although it feels very real, the sense of a permanent self is a fiction – created by energetic pulses – but a mightily powerful one. Our internal monologue overshadows our experiences, dwarfing everything and everyone else. We're in a prison of our own thinking, and it's so persuasive that we've convinced ourselves that it must be the truth. Our thoughts are like giants that loom over everything, separating us from others and the world.

Chapter 10
The Potential Centre

'Unity can only be manifested by the Binary.
Unity itself and the idea of unity are already two.'

THE BUDDHA

Your happiness depends on the degree to which your Potential centre is prominent, and how much its pulses are allowed to make you 'you' at any time. When – or if – that happens, you have an unshakeable sense of coming home, of being connected to everything and everyone. Fears dissolve, and your sense of isolation and separation is replaced by love and a sense of unity.

Although this is our ultimate birthright, it's possibly nothing more than a fleeting sense right now, and so we grasp for it as best we can through the pursuit of material gain and success in the world. It's always there, of course, as the silent witness to experience: the seer behind sight, the listener behind hearing.

The Potential Centre is the silent witness
when we're awake and when we sleep. It's the
only true source of a sense of self, although
paradoxically, it's not personal. It's the tool for
understanding the pulses from the other centres.

The Potential is also the centre of pure joy that's not affected by circumstances. We were it as a child, and we spend the rest of our life trying to get it back. Happiness is a poor approximate of joy, and we seek it in the world and through material gain as the other centres develop in and through time.

Eventually, as past hurts and bad experiences accumulate, we become time-heavy; rather, the sense of 'you' becomes more a vibration from the past. As it develops, so we develop a sense of a substantial self that's separate from the world. This self then needs to go out into the world in an attempt to discover happiness.

Yet, the 'you' that desires happiness is nothing more than a thought form, created from sensations of pain and pleasure, and the many fugue-like variations on the theme. The 'me' is given meaning and substance with the aid of narratives and belief systems that, in turn, create concepts through which we see and interpret the world.

These thoughts also determine the world in which you live and the boundaries you see in front of you. If you live by the belief system that tells you money doesn't grow on trees, you'll always have problems with money in your life. If you believe that the world is hostile – and this is a vitally important issue to examine in yourself – then people won't be friendly, and situations will invariably turn against you.

How can thinking be so powerful? On its own, it can't. However, it's your third centre – the Potential – that gives these thoughts power. The sense of unity and love comes from the pulses of the Potential, but it's also the field of all possibility, the creative source that'll make real anything on which you focus.

The Potential centre has been known by a variety of names by different cultures through the ages: consciousness, Atman, Nirvana, Mind, Krishna consciousness, the ground of being, the collective unconscious, the Field and God, among others. Whatever its name, it's consciousness, or the Potential centre itself, that makes all of life possible.

The creative power of the Potential centre is that which thinkers of the New Age refer to as The Secret, the Power of Attraction or manifestation. As described, it's a simplistic idea – that it's possible to think happy thoughts and have a million dollars mysteriously appear in your bank account. Invariably our wishes come from a place of unhappiness and dissatisfaction.

So long as we're unaware of the processes of Psychological time it's more likely that our ambitions and hopes are coming from the Past time-body as a reaction to a hurt or sadness.

There's no clarity when the three centres are each sending pulses – when we don't know which time-body is the dominant self, or when we're imagining a better future from a disappointing past. Only when these issues have been understood can we hope to harness the power of the Potential centre properly. Paradoxically, when we do, we want nothing else!

Our attempts to grasp just what the Potential centre is can be likened to a goldfish swimming around in its bowl and wondering what water is. However, unlike water that was put in the bowl by an outside agency, there's a paradox at the heart of the Potential centre: it is its own creator. It perceives itself into being and, in the perception, shifts from a field of potential and unity into a world of matter, multiplicity, and separate forms. It's the supreme observer, whose observations bring you, as a body and brain, into being.

The 'you' that isn't there

This is not 'my' Potential Centre, or consciousness, at all, but the universal consciousness made subjective. The Potential centre is not matter, but it manifests matter through the act of perception. It's outside of time and space, but creates both dimensions through the Present time-body. As such, your body is a space-time suit within its own creation, strange as that sounds.

The extraordinary truth is that you're a miracle because you're the eternal expressed in time, and the infinite appearing in space. Even this is not quite true – because there's no 'you' at all. There's the Potential centre, which finds expression through a body that you mistakenly call 'me'. There's no-space and no-time behind time and space. There's no-body behind you.

When the Indian sage Ramana Maharshi was dying from throat cancer, his dedicated followers were beside themselves with grief, imploring him not to leave them. A little puzzled, Maharshi asked his adherents where they thought he would be going, as there was nowhere he could possibly go. On his death, and on yours, the space-time continuum collapses, but you – as the Potential centre – go nowhere, because, without space, there's nowhere you can go.

When mystics say that you're not a body, they mean that you're the Potential centre, the unified field that has no separation or division, but only the appearance of such. Although you're fully ensnared in the drama of life, it's just the Potential centre unfolding. It's even a mistake to say it's all you – because there's no 'you' or indeed me, either.

Your body will die, and the graveyards are full of evidence of that; the Past, in time, will also die, but the Potential never dies, because it was never born, and the two events of birth and death happen in time. A body also moves in space, and the Past time-body travels with it, but there's no movement in the Potential centre. The ultimate truth is that you weren't born so you won't die, and although the drama of life appears to be going on, nothing is actually happening.

Although that's the absolute truth, an attraction between the Potential, or consciousness, and a body does take place; without it, the curtains couldn't go up, the lights wouldn't dim and the drama would never begin. And just as we become lost in a great film or compelling play, so we quickly forget that we're also the Potential centre, and we begin to identify solely with the body having its experiences.

This attraction explains why an inchoate sense of a 'me' starts to form as the first sensations of pleasure and pain occur when we're infants, and a division between the world and myself starts to manifest.

However, the sense of a 'me' as a feeling thing only truly develops with the rise of the Psychological past centre, the shadow self that sits between the Present and the Potential selves. This is the pull – and the tragedy – of the Past time-body. It knows the body just wants enough, but it also knows that the Potential centre is everything; the Past time-body's only expression is to want more, a pale imitation of the completeness of the Potential centre itself.

Only consciousness

Advaita is an esoteric branch of the Hindu faith. To its followers, it's the purest and truest expression of Hinduism and of all faiths. Its central philosophy also lies at the heart of Buddhism, and Zen Buddhism in particular. Put simply, it states that there's only one thing in the universe: consciousness. There's no you, no me, nothing but one thing. Because there's only consciousness and no 'me', even the idea of enlightenment is also an illusion because there's nobody to be enlightened.

However, although consciousness, or the Potential centre – the water in which the fish swims – is the absolute reality, just as important are the relative realities experienced by our Past and Present time-bodies. It's not enough just to be still and 'be' the Potential centre. If you want to live your life fully, and to do so every day, you have to see with great clarity the complex interplay between the three centres, and to observe which one is 'talking' at any time.

Each has its distinct pulse, and each will have its say, depending on the circumstances. One of the aims of this book is to help you identify each in turn. Sometimes several centres will try to speak at once, and, again, you need to differentiate and understand what's being said and by which centre.

The Hannah filter

In the world of time and space, 1+1+1=3. In the world of time and space, you have three centres. However, outside of this world, strange things start to happen to our mathematics: outside of time and space, $1+1+1 = 1$.

At death and before birth, you're the Potential centre, but from the perspective of time and space, this centre is unknowable. More precisely, it's beyond our knowing because that which is in time and space can't grasp that which is eternal and infinite. As your brain provides the framework for space and time, it can't begin to understand something that's outside of both. If you try to imagine infinity, you'll still see a wall. There will be a limit.

Outside of time and space, $1+1+1 = 1$, a phenomenon that I call the Hannah filter. It's named after the mother of Sir Isaac Newton, the celebrated physicist best known for his work on gravitational influences, who also examined the composition of light. Between 1665 and 1666, Newton carried out a series of tests that he called *experimentum crucis* (crucial experiments); in them, he demonstrated that white light is made up from a spectrum of colours.

From the one, many. From the unknowable one, multiple selves are created. Flip it around. Many also become one; the spectrum of colours collapses back into its originating single white light. Flip Hannah's name, and it still reads Hannah – it's the same thing, but read the other way round.

The Potential centre is the ground of all being, the creative force of the universe, which makes life possible. For the Christian Kant, it was the noumenon, or thing-in-itself without multiplicity; to the Buddhist it's Mind; to the Hindu, consciousness or Atman; to the Jew, the I-am-that-I-am.

While it's unknowable to the rational mind, which can formulate merely a concept of the Potential centre, it's something that's closer to you than even a thought. It's that which sees and hears, it's that which has been the constant observer while you're awake and when you sleep, from the moment of your birth – and before it, too.

Your body ages, but this is ageless; it 'feels' the same as it did when you were five years old. It's the 'I am' that begins every existential statement you make: I am hungry, I am tired. Although the 'I am' is never hungry or tired, it finds its expression through the body in time and space. In the stillness, you witness that which sees through your eyes, the consciousness that supports life and the room you're sitting in, the buzz of the fan, the birds singing outside, and the cars driving past.

It's clearly intelligent, but it also appears to be unknowing. It doesn't know itself. The only way a unified field could know itself is by creating itself as a multiple self. Therefore, your sense of 'you' as an isolated and separate being is a necessary illusion; it's necessary because if, like Toto in *The Wizard of Oz*, you lifted the veil and saw the Wizard for what he truly is, the show would end.

Perhaps you're not supposed to know that you're an expression of a unified field; perhaps, though, it's a process of returning home, but as a knowing and conscious being. 'You', as a sense of a separate self, come into being in relationship to the world and to others.

The Potential and the Present centres not only combine to create a world in time and space, but also become knowable only in relationship to this world, which seems to be outside of us or, more precisely, outside of our body.

Until we return home to the Potential centre, we're deluded and bewitched by this relationship, this dance between the outer and the inner, a dance that's enriched by our internal monologue, the narrative of our life and the pulses from the Past. As I've said, our thoughts are like giants – they make our internal landscape seem more real than any external one.

In this process, our sense of alienation increases, and we become convinced by the evidence of the senses that we're separate and alone. We're imprisoned within the cage of our body, sentenced to solitary confinement until the day we die – or until we awaken.

The move towards understanding

All of life is a movement towards understanding. That's why the Psychological past constantly seeks to relive an experience in order to finally understand it and so put it to rest. That's also why the constant endeavour of humankind throughout time has been towards an understanding of its world, primarily through the sciences.

Even the theory of evolution can be seen as an expression of understanding; yes, we seek to survive, and those of us who best adapt to our environment may be more likely to do so, but we've another thirst and hunger – for understanding and knowledge.

It's the one common factor that unites all of humanity across all time: we always seek to understand and to express our understanding – through the arts, mathematics, geometry and the written word, whether on a PC screen or a TV, on paper or parchment, on stone or on pyramids, or even on cave walls.

If the quest for greater understanding is indeed part of an evolutionary movement, the ultimate understanding that we're all expressions of the same unified field may be evolution's end.

Summary

It's extraordinary to realize that the true 'you' is, in fact, impersonal! You are consciousness itself, the silent witness or observer that's masked by the Past to create the drama of your life and the world.

Chapter 11
Understanding the Pulses

*'Home is where one starts from. As we grow
older the world becomes stranger, the pattern
more complicated, of dead and living.'*

T.S. ELIOT

Your natural state is a sense of being that has a focus around a metre in front of you. Although this is a pulse from the Present time-body, it's not body-centred. But then, the Present time-body incorporates the world and everything that's in it, including your body.

Then, perhaps, there's suddenly a pain in the stomach. The focus switches from its natural, resting state to the body, and the world loses its focus. The pain subsides, and a stranger walks up to me and asks if I went to such-and-such school. Now pulses from the Narrative centre take over as I recall my story. Happy with my answer, he says his farewells, but asks how he can get to a difficult location. Now the pulses from the Knowledge centre come into play as I try to recall how to get there.

Walking away from the stranger, I see in a crowd someone I think I recognize. I had a terrible argument with the person years before, and now the pulses from the Psychological past come rushing to the fore. And so it is that the pulses well up, creating thoughts and emotions, and, in that process, create a 'you' at any moment.

The voice – or pulse – of the Present is a quiet one, and we have to learn to be more sensitive to hear it. It will tell you when you need to eat (we all hear that one) and what it wants to eat. Unfortunately, once the Psychological past gets the message that food is required, it often takes over, and its pulse will start suggesting comfort foods that the body doesn't need – and that may even prove damaging – but which, as unfulfilled emotion, it desires.

The Psychological past extends in time the basic desires that come from the Present. This is often the reason why people who constantly struggle with obesity find it almost impossible to lose weight or to keep it off once it's lost.

Love is a sense of unity

To take another example, love is the ultimate expression of the Potential centre, because true love is a sense of unity. How many times have you been in love and felt that you were 'lost' in the other?

This sense of unity extends beyond your lover and includes the whole world and everyone in it. It won't last, however, because the Psychological past takes over with a myriad of thoughts and fears: *This is magical, but how long will it go on? I want to repeat this feeling again and again. I don't want to lose this person.*

Love, or the feeling of unity, is also timeless; being in love is a movement of the Psychological past and is in time – it asserts itself on the timeless. Eventually, this centre's fears and worries will corrode even the feeling of being in love, and will put in its place a different energy that'll eventually take the form of jealousy and insecurity but also care, tenderness and concern.

The Psychological past can have 'good' emotions, too, but they're pale reflections of the Potential centre itself. And none of these emotions is love.

The Present may be in time, but it doesn't live in Psychological time or create it; instead it merely provides the framework of space and time in which the drama of life may unfold. If the Present is threatened or frightened, it acts in the moment to protect itself. When the danger has passed, it ceases to concern itself with the problem.

However, the experience leaves a resonance in the Psychological past, as we've seen, and a simple event is extended and made substantial. The basic sexual need is extended by the Psychological past into lust or a craving for pornography, for example. It also begins to form your model of reality, so that one isolated event gets translated into a universal and eternal truth.

If the danger has a practical solution – such as fixing a broken stair – the Knowledge past will solve it. However, if there's nothing you can do, such as when you might feel insulted, the Psychological past often takes over.

It may start chewing over the event that has passed, and seek revenge, or find ways to avoid the danger in the future if you've been threatened. Either way, the experience lives on as a psychological reality, and the past event continues to have life, preventing you from being fully in the present moment.

When Jesus said that he, the Son (the Present time-body) and the Father (the Potential centre) were one, he'd overcome the Psychological past, as have all mystics throughout the ages. However, until we reach that understanding, each centre has an important function to play, and together they make you what you are. The tragedy of life is that the Psychological past holds sway — but it's a necessary tragedy.

From all that we've discovered so far, the question that probably keeps arising is the most basic of them all: why? If each of us is an individual expression of consciousness, of the Potential centre, why should we go through this painful process of misidentification?

Why can't we live simply in the miracle of the Present time-body? Why is the magnificence of the Potential hidden? Why, in short, are we living in hell when our birthright is heaven?

A return home

Throughout myth, there's the theme of homecoming, or nostos, a return to the place from where we started. References are found in books, poetry and drama, but probably its best-known portrayal is in Homer's *Odyssey*, and it's as bittersweet a return for Odysseus, our everyman, as it is for the rest of us. In that sense, we can never go home again, because we've changed. As the poet T.S. Eliot put it in *The Four Quartets*, we return to the same place, but we know it for the first time.

When we were infants and in heaven because we experienced no separation from the world, we didn't know we were in heaven, because we didn't then know the hell of separation. If we're in a place and don't know it, it's of little value. In that sense, we're unconscious. Therefore, if our natural state is heaven, we must know when we're there, and the only way to reach heaven is to pass right through hell.

It is we who have to finish the biblical myth of Adam and Eve. That's our quest – to return to the Garden of Eden as knowing beings who've tasted the fruit of the Tree of Knowledge of Good and Evil, who know it for what it is, and who've awakened from its hypnotic spell. Consciousness is a self-knowing process, and we play our part in creating a knowing universe. That's why each of the Three Selves is important – even the Psychological past, as it plays a significant part in helping us to become conscious.

So how do we break the loop and have the experiential moment? This is the reward of the Time-Light programme, outlined in the next section. An important part of the process is true forgiveness. To see the totality of any experience is to forgive the situation itself and the players in it.

The very seeing of something totally is the very act of forgiveness, and it naturally flows from that understanding. That forgiveness should be extended to you as well, because the idea of 'me' is no more or less substantial than the concept of 'others'.

In that moment of clarity, the narrative tape is wiped clean, and the concepts and beliefs supporting it crumble. This is possible only in moments of great stillness, when the three time-bodies coordinate. You're fully conscious and because one of the centres is outside of time and space, even the past can be relived in vivid detail – and forgiven. From then on, every situation is vibrant, alive, and changing in a constant present moment, and nothing can be encapsulated within a concept – not even you.

True forgiveness

Although many in the New Age talk about forgiving, forgiveness without understanding is hollow. If you forgive because you think it's the right thing to do (as you've been urged to do since childhood) rather than because you have a total understanding, you're still holding on to the resentment.

Those of us of a certain age may remember the scene in the BBC TV adaptation of Evelyn Waugh's *Brideshead Revisited* when a drunken Sebastian Flyte vomits through the open window of Charles Rider's ground-floor student rooms and contritely tells his new friend: 'To understand all is to forgive all.'

Whether he knew it or not, Sebastian was quoting an old French proverb, *Tout compendre c'est tout pardoner*, and it has the ring of spiritual truth about it. Although we can't know everything, we're able to use our own limited experience to empathize with the plight of another and so understand the situation. For the briefest of moments, we switch off the unconscious narrative in order to understand somebody else. In that moment of empathy, we're conscious.

The man who was able to forgive

John and Joyce live in upstate New York. They have one daughter, Jamie. When Jamie was seven, she heard the shattering news that she'd failed her entrance exams to a new school. All her friends had passed. Devastated, she ran up to her room and collapsed on the bed. Her parents rushed up after her, and reassured her that it didn't matter, that it was just a silly exam.

'The unspoken issue was that she felt she was stupid. She had learning difficulties, and she knew she couldn't keep up with her friends in the classroom. But we never dealt with that, and it became the first lie between us. After that, it felt that there was a space between us and Jamie,' John recalled.

But the problem went deeper. As a child, John had also experienced learning problems, and in the tough environment of his family, he was often reminded that he was 'stupid'. Although this all happened many years ago, the feelings were still raw, and John didn't know how to cope when he was confronted with the same problems with his own daughter.

Worse was to follow. Jamie became increasingly distant. By the time she was 13, John and Joyce started to suspect she was drinking. Again, it was something they didn't want to confront or deal with, and they hoped that somehow the problem would just go away. Again, it went deep for John, whose own father had been an alcoholic.

Eventually, Jamie moved on to drugs when she left home for university, and John and Joyce felt hopeless, shut out of their daughter's life.

Then, one day, Jamie was on the phone, sobbing, telling them that she'd been raped. John and Joyce drove through the night and reached their daughter by the morning. 'We couldn't believe what we saw. She was thin, she looked a mess, she didn't look like our daughter,' said John.

John had seen enough. He knew he had to tackle his own demons if he was to win back his daughter. 'We knew we had to do something, and so we received some counselling. I just instinctively knew that the only way out of this mess was forgiveness. I had to forgive myself, my parents, and Jamie' he said.

His forgiveness was severely put to the test weeks later when Jamie was living with them again. Jamie gave him a note she'd received from her drug dealer. She had to pay up or she would be killed, it said.

John went to meet the drug dealer with the money and a note of his own. In it he said that he knew the drug dealer was capable of better, that he knew he didn't want to hurt his daughter. He gave the note and the money to the dealer and left.

Two years later, in an Alcoholics Anonymous meeting Jamie was attending, the drug dealer revealed that his life had changed the day a stranger had handed him a note.

Forgiveness saved the drug pusher, John, Joyce and Jamie. It had wiped clean the past, and the patterns stopped. When John healed himself, he healed Jamie.

(From It Went Without Saying, Troy Book Makers, 2010).

The Sebastian Flyte moments are rare. We spend much of our time oblivious to the processes that shape our life and our day-to-day sense of reality. It's as though we sleepwalk through the day, unaware of the chattering of the narrative, of the filter of the Past through which we see the world, of the concepts we live by that support the beliefs that translate our experiences.

In turn, the narrative is created from experiences that are only partially observed.

The fully witnessed moment

A fully witnessed experience – one that's completely understood and observed – leaves no traces. When we're fully conscious, we not only see ourselves, but also the other people, the situation and the motivation that has created the experience. In that moment, we understand all and we forgive all.

As babies, we may not have understood that our mother didn't immediately tend to us at times because she was busy doing something else, not because she didn't love us. However, because we didn't have sufficient 'height' above the situation, these became the very first experiences of ours that were not fully understood. From that moment on, we started developing a feeling of separation from the world, and that wonderful sense of unity and oneness – from the pulses from the Potential centre – began to weaken.

Even so, the baby and the young child are still usually time-light, unless they've gone through a traumatic experience, and it's only with the passing years, when past experiences build and seek reiteration, that we become weighed down by time, until we see only the past and not the extraordinary 'now' of being alive.

Life becomes more difficult and less pleasurable until we feel separate or disconnected from the joy of living, which can be experienced only in the here and now. Most of us live through the there-and-then.

This movement from the Past centre reinforces the sense of time, taking us away from our very first feelings of unity with the world and our association with the Potential centre and towards the sense of a world that's 'out there', completely separate from us and over which we have little influence.

Nonetheless, out there's where we seek happiness, joy, and even spiritual fulfilment. We will never find it because the world out there is patterned by the past of unfinished business. We're like the dog that forever chases its own tail.

The Past time-body is therefore the source of the feelings that lie behind the concept that the world is separate from us, a sense that's subsequently reinforced by the sciences, which also work in a world that's separate from the scientist and us.

These feelings inform us of our world and of who we are. Unobserved and undefined, they form our assumptions about a separate world, and they give life to the fiction of a self as permanent and fixed. These are the 'mega-feelings' I mentioned earlier, because they create the metaphysical backdrop to our lives.

Unity, the ego and enlightenment

Through the ages, religions and spiritual practices have attempted to create unity in man, or unity between man and God (or the Potential centre). Yoga, for example, actually means 'unity', although the form that's practised most in the West these days is Hatha Yoga, the yoga of the body, which is merely a preparation for the main yogas. The four yogas of unity resonate with the world's main religions.

Karma yoga, or the yoga of selfless action, has its reflection in Christianity; bhakti yoga, the yoga of devotion, has hallmarks of Islam; raja yoga, the yoga of concentration and meditation, shares similarities with Hinduism; and jnana yoga, the yoga of knowledge and discrimination, offers many of the practices of Buddhism and Judaism.

Many other practices claim to help you reach unity. Some focus on the Present time-body – through deprivation, starvation or physical austerity – or on the Psychological past, often described as the ego. In the latter disciplines, you're encouraged to destroy the ego, or to stop thinking, through meditation and selfless acts.

While you remain unconscious to the constant pulses from the Past centre, you could no more stop thinking than you could stop breathing. Eventually you'll start thinking that you've stopped thinking! What matters is to see thoughts for what they are, where they come from and what they signify. It's like watching clouds passing over the sun. You still know the sun is there, and you know the clouds will pass.

Spiritual practitioners and gurus offer rituals and practices to still the mind, through mantras or prayer. Stillness is vital if you're to fall back in love with your life, although deep stillness comes about not from rituals or mind-deadening mantras, but from clarity about all of thought's processes.

Stillness occurs naturally, as you begin to recognize the movements, or pulses, from the Psychological past. That stillness is permanent, with a quality beyond anything achieved by ritual or even meditation.

It's also very important to understand the drive for enlightenment, liberation, or self-realization. Where does it come from, and what in us has that desire? The Present time-body has no need to be realized: it knows what it is. The Potential centre doesn't need to be realized because it already is that. This drive comes only from the Psychological past, from a desire to be more, to feel complete and fulfilled.

It may envision the state of enlightenment as a place of permanent happiness; if it does, this impulse comes from its own unhappiness. If enlightenment is seen as a state of complete serenity, it comes from its sense of agitation. If it thinks enlightenment is a place of complete fulfilment, it comes from its own sense of dissatisfaction.

Any attempt to suppress thoughts, kill the ego or starve the body derives from a sense of great unhappiness, agitation, or dissatisfaction, all of which begin as pulses from the Past centre, which get defined by the brain as thoughts, feelings and concepts. Desires for enlightenment and spiritual fulfilment are merely a continuation of those original feelings, which serves to strengthen the original thought further.

The ego is a necessary sense of 'I', born from the cumulative effect of three centres, so which ego exactly is to be destroyed? At the level of the Present time-body, the 'I' thought is necessary for the body to be fed and sheltered. At the level of the Psychological past, it's a vital part of the process of discovery. Consciousness, or the Potential centre, is just that: I, the only I in the universe, the I-that-I-am of the Old Testament.

It's important to see that all these concepts – of enlightenment or spiritual fulfilment – are merely more thoughts. Without those thoughts, you'd be happy, fulfilled and enlightened! The thought that you aren't experiencing any of these states is the only thing that stops them from coming into being.

Nonetheless, you're dissatisfied with your life, you've fallen out of love with it, and it's perfectly sane and rational to want something better. So if it's true that any movement towards happiness or enlightenment is only strengthening its opposite – the current state – what can you do? The journey back, your nostos, begins by truly seeing.

Summary

Every aspect of our lives is spiritual in the sense that everything we do is a quest to rediscover the Potential. It's true for the businessman trying to become a millionaire, the addict seeking the next fix and the monk who prays to see God. It's the same for all of us – to be at one with the Potential, or consciousness itself.

Chapter 12
Beyond Therapy

*'You could live in heaven, but you choose to
live in hell. The only question you have to
answer is: why have I made this choice?'*

What is the Time-Light theory? Is it a philosophy, a therapy, a self-help method, a way to reach enlightenment, or perhaps just a discipline to overcome depression and addiction? In a sense, it's all these things and more; it's greater, and deeper, than the sum of its parts. It's a new way to see yourself, the world, and the purpose of life:

- **It's a therapy** because problems such as depression and addictions are impediments to 'enlightenment' – shorthand for knowing that you're part of a unified field. But it's a therapy with a difference. It's not one of the 'talking therapies', which have their place as a short-term coping mechanism but don't always get to the heart of the problem. Time-Light is, instead, a 'silence therapy' because problems are made real and given flesh only through definition.

- **It's a philosophy**, but it has no value unless you're prepared to work with it in your everyday life. It's a self-help programme, too, but it isn't designed to deliver the usual prizes of wealth, more sex, fame, and the rest (although it might give you those things if you really want them).

- **It's about you, in your life, right now.** It tells you who you really are, and once you know that, everything else will follow. It tells you the truth about yourself before you die – so you can bring it into the world every day, which is your true purpose.

As we learned earlier, if you examine most therapies, their underlying assumption is that there's a 'you' that's the overlord, the commander that controls your thoughts – and is, essentially, 'the real you'. This commander also suppresses 'bad' thoughts and emotions into a place called the subconscious. These bad thoughts are the suppressed side of yourself, pushed down into your psychological trash can.

One of the key messages of the Time-Light theory is that the 'commander self' – the supposed *real* you – is a fiction, along with all the other selves that emanate up from the Three Selves. There's no commander; instead, there's a continuous series of selves that take shape from the pulses that are always rising up to the Present time-body in order to be understood – not suppressed. These form the untrue story of you.

As such, emotions and thoughts are neither good nor bad. They're associated with experiences that are repeating in the Present time-body. They're not 'you' any more than the commander self is you. These emotions and thoughts are ripples on the waters of consciousness. Not only are they not suppressed, they also don't need a psychological Band-Aid or positive thoughts or affirmations.

When a pulse rises to the Present time-body, emotions, thoughts and concepts almost instantaneously attach themselves to it, which gives the pulse definition and energy. This complex interplay of thought, emotion and concept is consolidated into a picture or image – that's how memory works.

We visualize the past, and we see it as an image or a series of pictures. The process – from pulse to emotion/thought/concept to pictorial representation – fires the 'negative' emotions that were associated with the original, and partially understood, experience.

Anger, resentment, jealousy, hatred and fear aren't 'you'; *they're emotional associations with experiences that are repeating in the Present time-body*. And they repeat because they want to be understood; they're seeking their own end.

One perplexing thing about the Time-Light theory is how it came into being in the first place. As I explained, it was an immediate, and ready-formed, torrent. But what had triggered that? Was it the book I was reading at the time, or the years I'd spent studying philosophy? Was it somehow linked to the mystical experiences I'd had as a small boy?

I don't entirely know, but once it had been created I wanted to test it with a series of questions. One question that many of us share is: Why does there seem to be so much evil in the world? Why is there always a war going on somewhere? Then there are questions that you may have posed at some time: Why do we always want more when 'enough' should be sufficient? Why do so many starve and a few have excess?

The golden thread

There's another question that I've toyed with over the years: Why is it that we don't 'get' the religious truths? Since we were toddlers, we've been taught the sayings of Jesus, Mohammed, Krishna or Buddha but, for most of us, they just haven't made that much difference to our life. Even those of us who observe the religious rituals and forms aren't really transformed by the teachings, it seems.

There are only two possibilities here: Jesus, Buddha and the rest are mad, in which case we're right to ignore them, or we just don't understand what they're saying. Looking around, there seems to be a gulf between their vision of the world and the world as it appears to be for us.

We're fed daily doses of news about muggings, murders, rapes and starving children, and the saints are talking about a heaven on Earth or a blissful state or nirvana. Looking at our own life, we seem to be making a mess of that, too. We might be divorced, or we have children we can't communicate with, or perhaps we have an addiction.

At the beginning, I asked the most fundamental question of them all: who am I? Although very few of us ask that question, it's the most important we can ever ask ourselves. I described it as the golden thread that would lead us to all the other answers.

I hope that I've demonstrated throughout this book that the who am I? question is, indeed, the master question, and its answer supplies the answers to all our other questions about life, and *our* life, that we may have from time to time.

You are the amalgamation of three energy centres that become more substantial in time and with experiences,

166

especially those that you don't fully understand. As such, understanding each centre and its characteristics and functions will provide the answer to all of our questions:

- There's evil in the world because we're more Past than Present and there's war when we fuse the Narrative past and its sense of identity in the world with the hurts of the Psychological past.

- We make a mess of our lives because we live on permanent repeat as the Psychological past tries to reach a final understanding of a hurt or sadness.

- We don't 'get' the religious truths because our Potential centre has become obscured by the pulses from the Psychological past. As most of us live that way, we've created a world that's a hell on Earth when it could be the heaven that our religious teachers promise us.

Spiritual truths are discovered only in life, in *your* life, and they're lived every day. The saint, guru or spiritual master who formulated the truths is at a different energy level to you. They're already time-light – and you're trying to understand what they say while you are time-heavy.

They might as well be speaking a foreign language and, in a way, they are. Because they've mastered themselves through time and you are burdened by time, you recognize nothing of what they say in your world. It doesn't make sense, and it doesn't even seem to be true. What could it mean to take no thought of tomorrow when you've got the mortgage to pay, or a child being bullied at school?

There's such a mismatch in the two visions of reality that, pretty quickly, you discard religion and spiritual teachings as so much wishful thinking or claptrap. Nonetheless, there will be times when you'll reach out for a holy book, or even decide to pay a visit to the local church or temple.

So what makes you do that if you've already decided it's meaningless? The same past-to-present movement that's messing up your life wants that mess – the misery or sadness – to stop. One remedy is the salve of religion and spirituality; another might be a car, or a new wife or husband. The ambition may change but the drive is always the same. It comes from sadness and regret – the yawning ache of despair at which we hardly dare look.

If we can't achieve spiritual fulfilment from a book, what's the point of reading any book, including this one? Books and words ready the mind much as a farmer tills the land in preparation for sowing, but true fulfilment is achieved only in action and in your day-to-day life.

The most important part of this book is not the theory, which we've now completed, but the experiential practice. This begins with the 21-day Time-Light programme that follows.

Are you ready to start unravelling the untrue story of you?

Part III

THE 21-DAY TIME-LIGHT PROGRAMME

Introducing the
Time-Light Programme

That to which you don't fully attend will weigh you down

If you bring forth that which is within you,
Then that which is within you
Will be your salvation.
If you don't bring forth that which is within you,
Then that which is within you
Will destroy you.

THE GNOSTIC GOSPELS

In order to complete the Time-Light programme you'll need a log to record your thoughts and observations, and a pencil. Buy a lined notebook containing approximately 100 pages – ideally, it should be A4 size (8 by 11 inches) because you've quite a bit of writing to do, although one half that size is more portable. If you decide on a smaller format, you may need to double up on some of the pages, in which case you may want a notebook with approximately 150 pages.

How to complete the exercises

There are 21 exercises in the programme. An arrow ▶ indicates the start of a new exercise, and one that you're to repeat every day until the end of the programme. Although we'll be adding a new exercise on each of the 21 days, each day you'll be repeating any exercise that has the ▶ symbol.

This means that you'll do the first exercise, 'Just looking', 21 times! Time-Light is a cumulative programme, and so you'll be carrying out the best part of 21 exercises on the 21st and final day. Onerous as this may sound, it's easy in practice because each exercise will take only a few moments to perform.

The purpose of the first few exercises is to learn simply to observe the pulses from the three centres. Don't give them strength by thinking or by embellishing them with feelings or concepts. Without the momentum of the conceptual brain, the pulses will remain just that – and will dissipate. As the pulses from the Past centre weaken, those from the Potential centre will come through more clearly. You'll realize that you're an expression of an eternal, unified field.

When you're doing this work, don't judge. There's nothing bad or evil about your thoughts: they are as they are. Any judgement is just another thought-form, and one that will send you right back to sleep. It's also important to do this work without expectation.

Don't carry out the exercises in the hope you'll get something out of this process – that you'll become enlightened or be happy forever. Letting go of expectation is tough because your entire mental makeup is predicated on the concept of effort/reward in time; you do something because you want something else.

This is another trap. If you expect a reward, you're projecting a thought-form into time: 'If I do this today, I shall be enlightened tomorrow.' Can you see that this very process is the problem? While you're in Psychological time – or, more precisely, when the pulses of the Psychological past dominate – you can't be in the here and now, and if you're not in the here and now, you're unconscious.

All of this seems difficult while you think about it – because your thoughts can't know any different – but it becomes simple and natural in the doing. What could be easier than to truly experience something with all your senses? What is so hard about writing down what you've just thought – and doing so without judgement?

Is it really impossible to change your tape and begin telling yourself something positive? Of course, you'll become unconscious again, and the narrative will start playing – but then you'll wake up and realize what you've been doing. Each time you wake up, you become a little more conscious, and that muscle will get a little stronger.

Day 1 ▶ Just looking

●○○○○○○○○○○○○○○○○○○○○○○○○○○○

Today we're going to relearn the ability simply to observe without interpretation.

In pencil, write 'Day 1' in the top left-hand corner of the first page of your notebook. Then write the words 'Just looking' in the middle.

None of us looks. We may look to cross the road or to see what's on the menu or to read our emails, but these are cursory forms of looking, just enough to get the required information. However, since the time when you were very young, you haven't really looked at anything purely out of fascination and curiosity.

By *really* looking, I mean absorbing yourself in something else with no thought of gain or power. Truly looking is the pure, undiluted act of observing without interpreting or imposing concepts. Once your conceptual mind has defined that which is being observed, you cease to look. If you really look at a flower, you see the utter mystery of it, and it is indeed mysterious when you get past the shorthand definition of 'it's a flower'.

Therefore, our very first lesson on day one of our voyage to the true story of you is to relearn the ability to observe. I mentioned a flower as an example, so let's start with that (it could be anything, of course).

Find time today to look at one flower in your backyard or garden; just one, but really, truly study it. Look at it for minutes, visually devour it, soak it in until the space between you and the flower *disappears*. Now I've just told you that will happen, you'll be waiting for 'the moment' – but it will still happen. You'll soon see that you've never really looked at a flower before.

You can do the same with your partner or a friend. Really, really look at their face (it's probably a good idea to mention what you're about to do beforehand), and you'll see things you hadn't noticed before. Truly! It will happen. Or over a meal, really taste the food in your mouth – its texture, its taste, its aroma.

In these moments when time itself seems to freeze, minor miracles may occur. 'You', for instance, may disappear for a while into the face of your partner, the taste of the strawberry in your mouth will be all that's in the universe for that short while.

Better yet, thoughts of work, the new car and so on will vanish – and you'll see that you are perfectly at peace in that instant of complete absorption. In that moment, you'll see with great clarity, without peering through a screen and filter. When you look at that flower, the space between you and it disappears, and with it all the possibility of unhappiness and misery.

Day 2 ▶ Thought-watching

●●○○○○○○○○○○○○○○○○○○○○○○○○

Today we're going to exercise stillness so that you can observe thoughts and feelings.

Start a new page in your notebook, and write 'Day 2' in the top left-hand corner. You need to split the page in two, so draw a line across it. In the top half, write 'Just looking' – because I want you to observe something different today – and in the bottom half, write 'Thought-watching' because that's the new exercise we're carrying out today. Today's and yesterday's exercise are to be repeated every day for the rest of the programme.

The purpose of this exercise is to get you back in touch with your natural inheritance, and to fall back in love with your life. You've fallen out of love with your life because you are living unconsciously, and according to a series of beliefs and concepts fuelled by a Past that seeks to relive experiences.

Mega-feelings (see chapter 4) have created a series of foundation beliefs – these include a belief that there's a world 'out there', that you're a separate being, and that you'll find happiness or fulfilment in that world.

You may have supporting beliefs that reinforce your world view – the world is hostile, it's every man for himself, money doesn't grow on trees, and he who dies with the most toys wins (rather than being the biggest baby, presumably). You may not be aware of these beliefs, and you might even deny them if you were challenged; nevertheless, the Past will invariably control the rational brain. Emotions always win out in a battle with logic.

We've seen how these beliefs have developed from experiences that occurred when you weren't fully conscious, triggering an emotional narrative from the Past self that seeks completion. That narrative creates images which, in turn, have helped establish concepts that are invariably universalized so that 'all Xs are Y'.

Forgiveness is a natural endpoint of understanding, and in forgiveness concepts vanish, as an emotional journey from the Past reaches its final destination. However, forgiveness flows naturally from a complete understanding; it doesn't have to be forced. We've also glimpsed what it's like to live consciously, and the wonderful stillness and expansion of space that happens when you do.

That stillness happens when you're conscious – when the Potential centre is allowed to become dominant and to co-ordinate with the two other time-bodies. But this sense of stillness is like a muscle. It needs to be frequently exercised, or you'll fall back to sleep and become unconscious again. When you're unconscious, the pulses from the Past self start up again.

Exercising stillness

So we need to start exercising stillness. From today, and for the next 19 days, I want you to write down some thoughts and feelings you have or, more exactly, thoughts or feelings of which you're *aware*.

This will happen after the fact; when you're thinking, you *are* that thought and so there isn't a 'you' that can observe it!

You have many, many thoughts and feelings throughout the day, from 'I'm hungry' to 'I don't like him'. Don't worry, you won't fill the notebook – you won't stay conscious often enough to record each thought and feeling you have.

This exercise is immensely subtle. As I've explained, an energy pulse that comes from one of the Three Selves precedes every emotion and thought. Initially, you won't sense the pulse itself, but I want you to start waking up enough to the thoughts and the feelings that follow it. It's a little like catching wisps of smoke as the feelings scud across the Present centre, and you have to be very still if you're to succeed.

In these initial stages, you may like to meditate first in preparation for this exercise. If you already meditate, and you have a technique with which you're comfortable and familiar, stick with it. If you're not a regular meditator, you might try a method that I like.

- Begin by sitting comfortably in a chair. Make sure your back is straight and your feet are planted firmly on the ground. Rest your palms in your lap and close your eyes. Take a deep breath in, hold it for a few seconds, and then slowly release it.

- Breathe in and out slowly five times. Now move your attention to the tip of the nose until you feel it tingle. If you can't feel anything, don't worry. You just need to become a little more still, so carry on breathing deeply.

- After a few more breaths, return your attention to the tip of your nose. Wait a few moments and you should start feeling it tingle. Now move to your toes, and again you should be able to feel a similar sensation. Repeat the process as you go around your body, to your fingers, your lips, your knees, your arms, and so on.

- Now just attend to the stillness itself. Thoughts may enter, but don't resist them. Let them pass over. Every so often, breathe deeply four or five times.

- Then smile. Not a manic grin – just allow your mouth to turn up slightly. If you can maintain a degree of stillness, meditate for 20 minutes. If you start to feel uncomfortable, or your mind becomes increasingly distracted, stop the meditation.

Now you may feel better able to watch your feelings and your thoughts. As you do so, just write them down, as a reporter would when writing the proceedings of a court case. It's important not to judge, criticize or condemn – those are also thoughts. It's not your job to discriminate between thoughts. A thought about God is not qualitatively better than a thought about a car; it's just another thought.

As you recognize this, you'll see that the narrative from the Past gives thoughts a value or weighting. That's why 'you' think one thought is more significant than another is. You'll soon realize that you can't hold the stillness for very long. As I say, stillness is a muscle that needs to be exercised, and in the early stages, you'll be amazed just how quickly you lose attention and drift off back into the reverie of your narrative, your untrue story.

Take your notebook to bed with you. Just before sleep is a good time to record your feelings and thoughts. Leave the book by your bedside in case you wake in the night and want to write something down. The more you do this, the more this will happen. Remember, it's an internal audit – not a 'things I did today' diary. It's there to record your interior landscape, and it's one of the first steps on the road to the miraculous life.

Day 3 ▸ Addictive behaviour patterns

●●●○○○○○○○○○○○○○○○○○○○○○○

Today we're going to look at our addictive and habitual behaviour patterns.

Write 'Day 3' in the top left-hand corner of the page. Split the page into three. Write 'Just looking' in one section, 'Thought-watching' in another, and 'Addictions' in the third. In a small subsection of the 'Addictions' area, write: 'What I did differently today.' You'll soon need two pages per day.

From today, we're going to work on our addictive and habitual behaviour patterns. All of the exercises outlined in this programme work together, and by doing them every day you'll start noticing that you're becoming more conscious anyway.

All unconscious behaviour and patterns will start correcting themselves (and I'm using 'unconscious' here to mean thoughts and feelings of which you've not been aware, not those that come from a subconscious or unconscious place). That's the key to everything we're doing – becoming time-light is a self-correcting process which unfolds naturally.

We're all addicts. Even if you don't drink, smoke, gamble, or have a sexual problem, you're still an addict. You're addicted to patterns of behaviour as the Past continues to replay itself through your Present time-body.

Eventually we become like a vinyl record – assuming you're old enough to appreciate the analogy – and the needle has created a groove which becomes deeper and deeper. As a result, we keep on playing the same old tunes. The deeper the grooves become, the harder it is to move the needle onto a new track.

Sometimes we can't do anything about our habitual behaviour – we have to be at work at a set time, for instance – but most times, we can. When we become more conscious, we stop telling the same jokes, making the same remarks and thinking the same thoughts.

Anything you try to change about yourself will fail or not sustain itself for more than an hour or two. That's because any effort with an end-point or aim in mind is yet another thought process; you're merely replacing an old pattern with a new one.

In the world of time and space, all of thought is predicated on the assumptions that there's a world out there, that the world out there has a solution or an ultimate prize, and that through effort and time, we'll attain that special prize. So, however you dress it up, or endow it with a quasi-spiritual name, it's the same process of effort ending in reward.

To break that mental habit, all we're going to do next is observe and record – and, occasionally, say our observations aloud so that they lose any power they might otherwise have from being silently, or tacitly, permitted (as you'll discover later in the programme).

Recording habits

So, from Day 3 onwards, we're going to observe and record habitual behaviour patterns. They won't be hard to spot, because virtually everything we do, say, and think is habitual; while we remain unconscious to the movement from the Past to the Present time-body, we're the vehicle for the past, which is where habitual behaviour lives. If you're conscious and present in the moment, you can't have habitual behavioural patterns; when you're present, the past can't be.

Right now, you're going through a programme of waking up, which means that you're not yet fully conscious. You'll keep 'falling asleep' to the hypnotic drumbeat of the past, but, as I hope you're beginning to see, it's not important that you fall asleep again, but that you know when you have.

With this new exercise, as we attempt to observe our thoughts objectively, we'll try to recognize patterns of the past. Every thought that's not problem-solving is from the past. However, I want you to do more than just observe and record. I want you to *act*:

- Every day I want you *to do just one thing differently*. It could be a minor change, such as buying a different newspaper, taking a slightly different route to work, having a filter coffee instead of a cappuccino, not putting butter on your toast, or going to bed at a slightly different time.

- The point is to do so consciously – and record the fact in your notebook. You could even recite to yourself: *I'm doing this because I've consciously chosen to do so*. It's important that you remember to do something different every day. Each time you do, you make those memory grooves a little less deep.

Most of us also have more serious addictions – ones that you'd call a real addiction – but the process is often the same. In some types of addiction, especially with alcohol and drugs, there's usually a biochemical element, and this needs to be addressed separately (see Day 10).

As we've learned, addictions come from the Past self, and are often an attempt to recreate an ecstatic moment. It happens while you are having a cigarette, a glass of wine, or a piece of cake, for instance. These associative thoughts – *I had the ecstatic moment when I was once drinking a glass of wine* – come about from a time when you weren't fully conscious to the moment and so were not awake to all the implications.

The Past has invested the thing with a quality that's fictitious but nonetheless convincing. For that moment, you genuinely believe that the glass of wine is somehow the cause of the moment of ecstasy. As a result, the Past develops cravings for a repeat of a pleasurable moment, which it believes is achieved if it repeats the action – such as smoking or drinking – in the same place or at the same time.

Because all this was going on while you were unconscious, a behaviour pattern established itself in the Past centre. The wrong association was created. Had you been conscious at the time, you would have realized that the feeling of pleasure is, in fact, a sense of utter completeness, an at-oneness-with-everything that emanates from the Potential centre.

In that case, the cigarette or the glass of wine wouldn't have taken the credit, and you wouldn't have started to develop a craving and an addictive behavioural pattern that would continually seek to repeat the experience.

As you become more conscious, the sense of oneness will become more common and, because you're more conscious, you won't associate it with whatever you happen to be doing at the time. You may be drinking, you may be smoking when you experience this sense of oneness, but you'd have experienced that feeling no matter what you were doing, and this you'll see as the programme develops.

Again, you'll realize that the whole movement from the Past time-body is predicated on the assumption of a world 'out there', and one that offers complete happiness or some ultimate prize. An addiction is merely a desire, based on a wrong association, which seeks to replicate a feeling of completeness, fulfilment or happiness.

Day 4 ▶ Thought-locating

●●●●○○○○○○○○○○○○○○○○○○○○

Today we're going to look at where our thoughts come from.

You need to start a two-page spread each day from now on. Write 'Day 4' in the top left-hand corner of the page. Now we need to create four sections across the two pages. Write: 'Just looking' in one section, 'Thought-watching' in another, 'Addictions' in the third (with a small subsection of this area called 'What I did differently today') and now 'Thought-locating' in the fourth section.

An energy pulse precedes every thought, but the movement's so subtle that it may take a while before you see this. Without interpretation by the brain, a pulse wouldn't gain energy or definition, but instead would dissipate. However, while we're unconscious to the process, concepts, thoughts and past hurts quickly attach themselves to the pulses and give them life.

Most people say it's the other way round, that thoughts spark feelings – and it's certainly the case that thoughts *strengthen* the feeling – but all the thoughts and emotions you have that make you a 'you' as a thinking being begin with the pulse. Once that process has started, the emotions and thoughts act as a catalyst for more pulses.

After all, you had feelings long before you could think or formulate words and simple sentences, as does every newborn. Eventually you learn to express that subtle pulse – sometimes it's a torrent or an uprush – and to put it into words. We've been doing this for so long now that we rarely notice that the words are a poor approximation of that feeling. We have just a handful of broad brushstroke phrases that are clumsy expressions of something so much more subtle, so quicksilver.

The exercise of keeping the notebook is the first stage in developing the ability to sense pulses without defining them as thoughts or emotions, to feel the pulse as it ebbs and flows. Disconnected from words, the pulse loses its potency because it is, quite literally, indefinite – it hasn't been defined. Ultimately, that which you don't define can't sustain itself in space and time; deprived of its definition, it loses its energy.

As you become still, so you attend. However, just as a toothache disappears the moment you sit in the dentist's chair, so emotions and thoughts subside when you're watching and waiting in stillness. Eventually, you'll fall asleep once again and the narrative will take over, but note in your log each time it happens.

Watching the pulses

For this exercise, I'd like you to start calculating from which self the pulse comes. To begin with, it'll be just a guessing game, but you'll get better and better at it the more you do this exercise. The thought or feeling will rarely arise from just one time-body: it'll be an admixture from more than one of the centres.

For example, the sudden thought of eating comes initially from the Present time-body as a pulse for food but is quickly embellished by the Past centre as a need for comfort or reward food, such as a large slab of chocolate cake!

Here are a few parameters to help you gauge how the thought and feeling have come into being:

The Present time-body has basic needs for shelter, rest, safety, exercise, nutrition and sex. It also has basic emotions that are directly associated with the body, such as fight or flight, and fear of an immediate danger. The brain is also a part of the body. It can solve problems and it has the remarkable ability to think conceptually, which includes the imagining of things in space and time.

The Past time-body sits between the Present time-body and Potential centres, and it can be pulled in either direction; it increasingly identifies with the drama of the world as its narrative begins to become dominant. Fundamentally, the Psychological past is the Present time-body writ large. The Present time-body wants 'enough' and sufficiency − it wants sufficient shelter, enough money with which to live, enough food.

The Past time-body wants more, much more than the body actually needs. This is because the drive for more is the only expression that approximates with the Potential centre itself, which is infinite and eternal. While anger is an emotion from the Present time-body in response to an immediate threat or challenge, hatred derives from the Past centre because it's a continuation of anger in time.

The Present time-body may desire sex, but the Past self will experience lust, sexual deviancy, and even an interest in pornography, as these feelings are an extension of the basic sexual urge in time. The Present time-body may have a sudden feeling of fear, but it's in the Past self that you find phobias.

However, not all feelings are negative. The Past time-body is also capable of feelings of affection, kindness, care, concern, sympathy – and its highest attribute, empathy. Again, these are extensions in time of basic feelings registered in the Present self.

The Potential centre, too, is part of the mix of 'you'. Like the Past time-body, the Potential centre sits outside of time and space, but unlike the Past centre, it doesn't reinforce the sense of time and space generated by the Present time-body.

The highest expression of the Potential centre is pure love, which is the sense of unity. Despite what most people think, hate is not the opposite of love, although feelings of hate do arise from a sense of disunity and separation. Love has no opposite – the closest negation is a lack of love, a sense of isolation and separation.

A feeling of completeness may come from the Potential centre, but the Past time-body can subvert this into a great yearning. Similarly, the sense of unity can be translated by the Past self into a need for religion or contemplation. The Past time-body's feelings of general dissatisfaction and a need for more are not a reflection of the Present centre, which wants just enough, but of the Potential itself, which is everything.

A quantum physicist might describe the Potential as the field of all possibilities. As the Potential is not defined, and nor is it in space and time, it remains a potentiality in relationship to the physical world. It's important to grasp that the Potential is a creative force, a potential for every situation occurring in time and space. That's why thinking and feelings are so important: they act as a vital framework that gives shape to the creative power of the Potential.

So putting that into practice, a basic bodily need, such as a feeling of hunger, comes from the Present time-body, whereas daydreams of a lavish feast come from the Past time-body. A sudden feeling of being 'at one' or complete is an expression from the Potential centre, whereas fear, or a sense of isolation, is from the Past.

Have some fun with this exercise, and with the thousands of thoughts you have every day. You won't catch most of them as they fly across your mind, and most of the time you won't even notice you're thinking, but when you do become aware of a thought, try to figure out the centre from where it has come.

You could even carry out this exercise retrospectively. Suppose that you were thinking this morning that you really didn't want to go to work today because you have that meeting to attend – which centre would have such a thought? Or you really hope that some individual doesn't get into your train compartment – which centre is that? I need to lose weight before the summer... my shoes are killing me... it's going to rain and I'm going to get soaked – how about those?

Working out where these thoughts come from is all part of becoming conscious, of slowing the narrative, of stopping the movement from the Past to the Present. All of thought is in Psychological time, a movement from the Past to some assumed future or to some imagined Present.

Carrying out this exercise correctly can be about becoming a child again, to a period when you were not so burdened down by time, when you were time-light. Now time weighs heavy because you've become time-heavy – rather, you've been submerged by the past and that which is dead and finished.

To unravel your untrue story, you must exorcise the ghosts of the past. The buzz of being is found only in the now, and the now knows nothing of the past or any future.

Day 5 ▸ Stopping time

●●●●●○○○○○○○○○○○○○○○○○○○

Today we're going to look at how Psychological time is a movement from the past.

Write 'Day 5' in the top-left corner, draw up the sections you created for Day 4, but leave space for today's exercise, which you should title 'Stopping time'.

The narrative from the Past time-body stands in the way of the buzz of being. While your life is a constant becoming – a moving to something better – you're not being, you're becoming. Only a human being, not a human becoming, can fall back in love with his or her life. In the last few days, we've done some exercises to slow that movement of time; today's exercise is all about stopping time altogether.

Do you recall the little experiment we tried on the very first day of the programme, when I asked you really to look at something – a flower in your garden or someone's face? If you did try it, you may have noticed that the space between you and the object disappeared, and it seemed that time stopped, too.

That's because a life that's fully conscious doesn't live by an unconscious narrative from the Past, but from the here and now, the vibrant Present. The here and now is clearly the only actuality – it can't be the half-remembered Past or some projected future – and so the only way to live is fully to connect with the present. When you see, hear, taste, smell, read the newspaper, walk in the street, and engage in the countless other things you do every day, you must do so fully.

We spend the day sleepwalking, or thinking – which, unless it's problem-solving, is the Past imprinting itself on the now. This imprinting is pervasive: whenever we see someone we've met before, we don't *really* see them at all but instead immediately impose a past image on them. When we look at a flower, it triggers a chain of thoughts about the fact that we need to do some weeding next weekend. When we see our office building, we think about the awful meeting we're due to have there today. And so it goes, all day, every day.

While the amount of imprinting we do almost every moment is extraordinary, the movement itself couldn't be simpler to observe; it's always from the Past to the future, bypassing the Present. That future could be just a few seconds ahead, but the imprinting can never be related to the current moment – because you're living that right now, even if you're not conscious that you are.

While thinking appears to happen in present time, it is, in fact, the movement from a half-experienced Past to an imagined future: you can't think about Present time until it's Past, even though it may be just a fraction of a second later. If you have a complete experience in the Present, there's no thought at all. We've all experienced that: at the point of orgasm, for instance, or during the scary moments of a roller-coaster ride.

During those moments, we're utterly at one with the Present, and because it's so rich and complete, we want to have the experience again and again. We let go of the desire for a repeat or replay of an ecstatic moment only when we're conscious of the process. Until we are, we'll continue to associate the extraordinary feeling with the experience itself, and so try to repeat it by replicating the circumstances.

You may experience an overwhelming sense of joy and completeness when you're in a friend's sports car, for example. This creates an energy print in the Past time-body that wants that experience again, and because it was an association with a sports car, you won't rest until you purchase a sports car for yourself. Somehow, a sports car is associated with happiness and joy, even though the feeling actually occurred because you were present.

Only when we're fully conscious does the process of past-creating stop. When we're not creating from the thought store of the Past, we don't project into a supposed future, and we're finally free to live fully in the Present.

Experiencing with all the senses

So far, we've been recording our thoughts and trying to understand from which centre they come. Now we're going to extend the little experiment we started on the very first day to see if thought can come to a complete stop, just for a little while. There's no force or coercion involved, and I don't want you to try, in the sense of making a big effort.

If you *try* to stop thinking, you'll attempt to do so because you imagine that there's a bigger reward at the end of the process – and that merely creates yet another line of thought. To stop thinking, we're not going to try to stop the process. Instead, we're going to fall naturally and easily into life, by absorbing ourselves in it, as we did when we really looked at a flower, as though we were seeing it for the first time.

This time I want you to experience your hand – again as if you've never properly seen it before (which, by the way, you probably haven't). With our first exercise on Day 1, I asked you just to *look* at a flower – I didn't ask you to touch it or smell it. Today, I want you to experience with *all* your senses.

- I want you to look intently at your hand, observe the fine hairs on its surface, the blue veins, the knuckles, the nails and cuticles. I'd like you to touch your hand; what does that feel like? Smell your hand. Be aware of the energy pulsing through your hand, the tingling of the fingers, the duller sense of the palm.

- Now close your eyes and really feel the hand with your senses fully alive. All of this took only a minute or so – but in that short time, you didn't think. Thinking just stopped naturally. For that time you were fully conscious. There was no narrative to accompany the observing and sensing.

When there's no naming, no narrative, the true mystery of all things reveals itself as something beyond words. Everything in the world is remarkable because it's mysterious. You can't know things in the way that your rational brain would like to comprehend; the thinking brain is in time and space, and the mystery of things sits beyond both dimensions.

You can freeze-frame time in this way with any object or thing. A tree is a good target; approach it as though you've never seen a tree before. Don't try to classify it or even name it as a 'tree'. Don't bring up memories you may have about it – it could be the tree your son fell from, but let such thoughts go.

Look at it from a distance so that you see it in its totality. Slowly walk towards it; now the very top may not be visible. Feel the trunk, the branches and the leaves. Just absorb the miracle of its life, of life itself – a life that's beyond words and thoughts, which is how life is in its true form.

You can freeze-frame anything at any time. Try to do so at least once every day. If you're at work, study your desk or your clothes; when you're on the train, look at the other faces or the smears on the window. When you walk home, look at the pavement as though you've never seen it before. See it as new and different.

Look without words, without thoughts, without narrative. Not only will you truly see, possibly for the first time, but you'll also be outside of Psychological time. The movement of Past to future will cease. The constant narrative of your life will fall silent. The Potential centre, your third self, will shine through.

Day 6 ▶ I am a camera

●●●●●●○○○○○○○○○○○○○○○○○○

Today we're going to introduce moments when we don't use concepts.

A new exercise for Day 6 – and by this stage you're likely to need an extra page, so each day henceforth will require at least three pages of note-taking. Begin by adding the new day in the top-left corner and then copying the sections you laid out for the previous few days. This time, however, we're adding a new section (for which the third page may be necessary), called 'I am a camera.'

The Past is the filter through which you see the Present, and its initial form of communication is an energy pulse, or uprush of feeling, which can be subtle or forceful. This pulse is almost instantaneously defined by the brain, with words and thoughts or feelings. This has the effect of strengthening the pulse; a pulse that's translated as 'angry' will make you angrier still.

Anger also comes from the Present time-body, but this is in response to an immediate situation with which the body is faced, and it's a natural, even healthy, reaction. However, as with the uprush from the Past self, the anger from the Present self is also quickly defined, at which point the feeling ceases to be in the moment, and instead becomes part of the Past.

This is a well-known phenomenon; it's often called 'becoming self-conscious'. The Present time-body reacts, and in that moment, your body is absolutely at one with the situation, but within seconds, a split occurs, and you almost see yourself being angry as if you were outside of the situation, observing yourself as a bystander would.

At that point, the process of 'anger-making' may stop – as it would if you were conscious of the process – or you may allow the brain's acknowledgement that you're angry to fuel the emotion and give it life beyond the moment, and beyond that which is necessary for the situation.

Sometimes, though, we become embarrassed by our behaviour when the split occurs. A new emotion may come into play to deflect from the original display of feeling, or we may apologize, wondering what came over us.

The split – that rare moment between an honest feeling from the Present time-body and the subsequent reaction that seems to take over – is a perfect example of two of the time-bodies functioning almost as one. The emotion shifts from the Present to the Past time-body, where it's sustained by a defining of the initial feeling. Without words and definitions, the pulse, or uprush of feeling, loses its energy. Such is the importance of words, thoughts and feelings: they keep alive the Past.

They're also vital, of course, as they're the lingua franca of the conceptual mind. We need them in order to make our way through the world, to create things and to make life more comfortable or easier. When the conceptual mind is problem-solving, it's functioning healthily. However, the conceptual mind is like a child with attention deficit disorder on sugar: it just doesn't know when to stop.

It creates concepts about everything, as we've already seen. Your body is a concept, as is time and space, the 'world' and your place in it, and indeed everyone you meet. It's almost impossible for you to see anything any more except through a concept, and, as a result, we don't really see anything at all. That's why, in an earlier exercise, I invited you to freeze-frame life, and really experience things that are in front of you.

Another important aspect of freeze-framing is to witness without words. Words not only have the dual function of fuelling concepts and giving life to a pulse from the Past timebody, they also make possible the constant commentary and meaningless jabber that broadcasts to you every moment.

Seeing without words or reference

So part of becoming conscious – of discovering your untrue story – is to live and experience without words and definition. Although words are a constant companion in your life, you'd be astonished by how little you need them. For this exercise, I invite you to switch them off.

When the writer Christopher Isherwood coined the phrase 'I am a camera' in his book *Goodbye to Berlin* (1939), he meant that he was merely a lens, recording whatever was in front of him, without comment or judgement, and that's a good description of our next exercise. I want you to become a camera, sweeping around a room or office, just observing, but without words.

When your eyes alight on a television set, don't record 'television set'; instead, just observe it as a something in the room. The same goes for everything that enters your field of vision: a tree ceases to be 'a tree', but is just a large shape with certain smells and features that you experience. As the Bible suggests, be like a stranger in a strange land. You don't know the name for anything you see, you don't know what's in front of you, other than the obvious fact that something is.

That way you'll connect directly with the person or object in front of you. Instead of seeing it through a lazy label – a tree, a bird, a cloud – you see it for what it truly is, in all its magnificent mystery. A tree is not really 'a tree' – which, after all, is merely a word or concept – it's a mysterious something, and the same goes for everything you witness every day.

To do this properly, you need to be quiet, and you need the time. It's not a great moment to try this when you're rushing to get the children to school or catch the train to the office. Instead, choose a moment when you have the time, when you're sitting down in the evening on the train or in the car.

As with all these exercises, the important thing is to do a little every day. You can perform this exercise in a minute or so, and can extend it until you're able to maintain it for an entire evening. For example, you could watch television without using words or defining what you see. You could tune out the words being spoken by the actors so they become meaningless to you, just a wash of sounds, as if they were playing musical notes instead of speaking.

Once you've carried out this exercise a few times, you'll see just how marvellous your brain truly is. It switches to words and concepts the moment they're required – to problem-solve or to deal with some issue that's arisen – before returning to camera mode, its natural resting state.

The more you consciously switch to 'camera', the more it will begin happening naturally by itself without any prompting.

Before long, your brain will be retrained to work, as it should, responding as necessary instead of as the chattering monkey it is right now.

Without words, the space between 'you' and the 'world' will shrink and there will be no division between subject and object, you and the world – because you'll cease to be the pivotal point of reference. A more accurate – and clumsier – expression of this state is seeing that there's no division.

So get your camera rolling.

Day 7 ▸ Changing the tape

●●●●●●●○○○○○○○○○○○○○○

Today we're going to look at how our thoughts create us and the world we live in.

Another new exercise, for Day 7 onwards. You really will need that three-pages-per-day format now! Write 'Day 7' in the top left-hand corner, copy the sections from Day 6, this time adding a new section on page three – 'Changing the tape'.

Our thoughts create our world. They're based on unexamined assumptions about the world and ourselves, which are themselves created from partially observed experiences. These thoughts, feelings, and assumptions are given potency by the third body, the Potential, the field of all possibility.

Although we almost never become conscious of them, our thought narratives are a conjunction of beliefs. You might maintain that life is hard, money doesn't grow on trees, and you have to push if you're going to succeed in life.

All these beliefs are interpretations of past events that were never fully understood – or were narratives started by parents, teachers or friends that we've absorbed. Something happened at a certain time or your parents told you something when you were at an influential age, and it started a narrative running.

Consequently, we walk around with these unspoken assumptions, busily discovering the world we've chosen to create. Money will always be hard to come by if that's what we've been told, and this becomes our truth for several reasons.

At the prosaic level, it's because the thought-forms ensure that there will always be difficulties about money and getting it, and this will further endorse an existing thought pattern.

We won't recognize any evidence that disproves the belief, even when we encounter it, because our focus while we wear the 'life is hard' spectacles will always be looking to confirm our initial belief. This is one of the hardest things to come to grips with: your life, for good or bad, has been your choice.

You're responsible, and to an extent that would startle you. You'll find whatever it is that you're seeking, and you'll live a life that's aligned with your thoughts. Although it's been an unconscious process, you've nonetheless decided to live according to a negative narrative. You are your own self-fulfilling prophet, usually of doom.

Creating a new narrative

Now that you know this, you can change the tape. First, look for a pattern in your life. Money might be an issue, or you may have problems maintaining a long-term relationship with someone, or difficulty with time-keeping. Whatever the pattern – and there will be one or more – it's a good indicator of your own narrative.

Let's assume for a moment that money is always an issue in your life. This suggests that the narrative you have running maintains that money is a scarce resource. So today, we're consciously going to change the tape. At every available moment when you remember, I'd like you to think: *money is easy to come by; it's in ready supply; there's never a lack.*

It'll be easy to do this the first few times, but you'll soon forget and fall back to sleep, hypnotized by your unconscious narrative. To help jog you awake, write down these thoughts in your notebook and put an elastic band or a piece of cotton around your wrist. As you do so, tell yourself that it's there to act as a reminder to look in your notebook.

If the first day isn't too successful, don't worry – do it again the next day. As with maintaining attention on the present moment, the conscious narrative is a muscle that needs exercising, and it'll get better the more you do it. As you do so, you'll start seeing examples in your life that suggest money is easier to come by than you used to believe. Acknowledge this new fact, which will give you fresh energy to continue with the conscious narrative.

There's no end to the positive narrative tapes you can play for yourself:

- Play one that tells you that you're a valuable and worthwhile person.

- Play one that tells you that you're talented and respected.

- Tell yourself that everyone is divine, and when you look into the eyes of another, you're looking at God.

It isn't that these positive narratives are necessarily any more 'true' than the negative ones. The belief that money grows on trees is no truer than the belief that it doesn't. It's what you determine to be true that matters. This exercise has nothing to do with absolute truths. As we've already seen, there are no absolute truths in our world of time and space.

Truth or reality has everything to do with choice. You choose to continue running the negative narrative, albeit unconsciously, or you begin to wake up and consciously change the tape. As the tape changes, so will your reality.

It's important that you begin looking out for small changes in your life, because they'll start occurring. Often, these signals of change were there before, but you just chose to ignore them because you'd already told yourself that life can't change.

When you witness these changes, be thankful for them and give yourself a little smile. After all, you've stumbled upon a most remarkable gift: that you're responsible. Although once this may have been the scariest thought imaginable, welcome it now because it's a power you can use.

Life will cease to be something that just happens to you and instead becomes something that you can begin to change and meld. Best of all, as you experiment with bringing change consciously into your life, you can have enormous fun. Remember, though, that conscious change is just a small part of waking up, and it's but one aspect of a much larger process starting to unfold.

Ironically, when you were unconscious, you may have wanted to be a Master of the Universe. Well, guess what? You are one.

Day 8 ▶ Dealing with resentment

●●●●●●●●○○○○○○○○○○○○○○○○○

Today we're going to look at the impressions from the past that we've accumulated about others.

As always, start a new page in your notebook. Write 'Day 8' in the top left-hand corner, copy across all the previous exercises and sections, and add the new exercise, 'Dealing with resentment'.

All of our exercises are about becoming aware of the movement from the Past time-body, and especially the Psychological past into the Present. Being aware is all you have to do. Any attempt or effort to change the pattern comes from the Past, which is constantly seeking resolution or a reward, such as enlightenment or never-ending joy.

Because of this movement, you're being short-changed. You're not living in the moment, but experiencing everything through a filter from the Past time-body: past feelings, past thoughts, past perceptions, past images.

We've seen that our feelings, thoughts, and perceptions filtered by the Past time-body begin with a pulse that's instantaneously translated into a thought or emotion. When you see someone whom you've met before, you've an immediate feeling about that person, based on your previous encounter with him or her. The true and honest response to any person or situation is a neutral one.

As everything is in a constant state of flux, the person and the situation are completely different from your previous encounter. Nevertheless, that's how it remains for you, as though the experience and the person were stuck in aspic.

Catching your feelings in flight

Your feelings about that person may range from mild indifference to a strong dislike, even resentment. Although I've called today's exercise 'Dealing with resentment', it concerns any emotion that's robbing you of the full experience in the Present.

As it's a new exercise, you'll probably start catching yourself having a feeling about a person or a place only after the fact. This happens because you're not conscious enough to be able to catch the emotion in flight.

So, to begin, it's enough for you to reflect back on a feeling you had, whether it was a few moments ago or an hour or more ago. Either way, don't worry – just record it in your notebook. Think of any occasion in the recent past when you felt some sense of resentment, hurt, anger, frustration or irritation. Write down the occasion, the details and your feelings about it. As with all these exercises, don't judge or condemn.

As you continue with this exercise, the time between an event and your realization of a certain feeling about it will shorten. You may start out becoming conscious of the feeling a full hour afterwards, but the more you do this, the shorter the time gap will become, until you become conscious in that moment. At that point, feelings and thoughts about any situation in front of you will stop naturally.

Day 9 ▶ Forgiveness + Gratitude

●●●●●●●●●○○○○○○○○○○○○○○

Today we're going to exercise our gratitude and forgiveness – but in a slightly different way.

A new day, a new exercise or two. Create a new three- or four-page log for Day 9, copy across the sections from Day 8, and add a new section on the third page: 'Forgiveness + Gratitude'.

Our work on becoming conscious is getting interesting. Your notebook should be filling up with some of the thoughts you've monitored and their origins, whether from the Present, Past, or Potential centres. You've also had a go at stopping Psychological time by experiencing with all your senses. You've looked dispassionately at something you held as true about someone. You've become a camera. And you've ejected your unconscious tapes, and instead installed and played some positive tapes of your own.

Today, I'm adding another two tasks to the workload. Every day henceforth, I want you to be grateful for something in your life, and I also want you to forgive someone.

Saying 'thank you' with meaning

Being grateful for something isn't so hard – or shouldn't be. The daily grind overwhelms us, and it's too easy to overlook the thousands of things for which we could be grateful every day:

- You can be grateful for your feet taking you to the train or the pavement for making your going easier.

- You can be thankful for the car that slowed to let you cross the street, or for your heart, which keeps beating.

- You can celebrate your lungs for breathing in and out, and for the air that lets you live.

- How about the food you're given every day, and your children, your husband or wife?

Whatever you choose, make it the subject of your conscious gratitude for the day. Write it down and date it in your notebook, and refer to it throughout the day.

But here's the thing – I want you really to *mean* it. This is not a form-filling exercise; your feelings should flow from the heart, and you should express your gratitude with passion. Feel your gratitude when you express it, ideally aloud.

If that's difficult, and you aren't alone when you're carrying out the exercise, at least say it with meaning to yourself. And when you say it to yourself, do so with a little smile on your lips as you think of that person or thing for which you're grateful.

Forgiveness begins by forgiving yourself

The other daily exercise is to forgive someone or some situation. This may be a tougher exercise than your gratitude notes because, as we saw in an earlier exercise, true forgiveness comes naturally only from complete understanding. However, if you're carrying out the exercises diligently, you're starting to wake up. It's worth pushing yourself to see if you can swim in the warm waters of forgiveness.

Our pride usually gets in the way of forgiving. We don't truly believe another person deserves to be forgiven; after all, he or she was awful to you. You suffered as a result – so why forgive? Here's why: by not forgiving, you've built more Psychological time, and that stands between you and falling back in love with your life.

Being resentful isn't hurting anybody but you. The person who harmed you isn't feeling that sense of resentment, is he? But you are. So not only did you suffer in the first place, you're continuing to suffer now and every day.

Although we're not conscious that we're still resenting someone or some past situation, that state of mind is the currency of the Past time-body; it's unconscious. Hardly a day goes by when somebody doesn't give us cause to get angry or irritated, especially when we're unconscious.

It could be from a careless motorist who drives in front of you, forcing you to stop, a work colleague who doesn't do something he promised, or your partner or spouse who says something that upset you. It might even be the man in the coffee shop, who served you the wrong sandwich.

One way of testing if there remains a trace of a past upset is to imagine the person or situation involved and sense if any pulse of energy, or slight uprising of feeling, occurs as a result. If it does, you still have an unconscious memory of the experience. You need to let it go – otherwise, this ghost of an experience will continue to haunt your Present, and you won't have a full connection to the here and now.

As you start the exercise, it's better if you begin with a relatively insignificant upset, such as the man in the coffee shop.

Whatever it is, write down the words of forgiveness in your notebook, such as:

'To the sandwich man, I truly and deeply forgive you from the bottom of my heart for giving me the wrong sandwich today. I'm releasing you, and I won't carry the burden with me. You're dissolved in my love.'

You can choose your own words, so long as you get across that meaning.

One important part of forgiving is adopting a wider perspective in order to understand why the event happened. In the case of the wrong sandwich order, the sandwich man was busy, and he forgot.

You can take the same perspective with the person who cut you up when you were driving. He may have been late for collecting his child from school and so was in a rush, and consequently misjudged the distance and your speed. These inconsequential events in your daily life offer you a great opportunity to hone your forgiveness skills.

Once you've tried this a few times, you'll see more and more opportunities where you can practise forgiveness. Interestingly, forgiveness is a movement of the Potential centre, and the more you wake up, the more the Potential will become part of your life. Waking up is a process of being present in the here and now, and, for that to happen, the Past must loosen its hold. But that can happen only when you become conscious of the Past time-body.

A partially observed experience becomes trapped in the Past time-body, where it continues to have a half-life, trying to complete itself. It wants resolution, and that's why the Past continues to live in you. The practice of forgiveness brings the old hurt back into your life, as if it was still happening, and completes it. Once completed, the energy dissipates and vanishes. Your burden is lighter and the here and now becomes more vivid.

Forgiveness and gratitude are processes for bringing you into the Present, and allowing you to start falling back in love with your life.

Day 10 ▸ Kindness to the animal

●●●●●●●●●●○○○○○○○○○○○○

Today we're going to make sure our body and mind are always properly looked after.

Although it's an exercise, Day 10 introduces a series of recommendations for keeping the body healthy. By this point, you'll need four pages per day. So copy everything across from Day 9, giving things a little more space this time, and then add a new section: 'Kindness to the animal.' This exercise is a one-off: do it only today.

You may already be carrying out many of the things recommended in this exercise – but write down anything new that you can introduce to make your body healthier.

It's time to move our focus from the Past time-body, where all our efforts have been concentrated so far, and to give a little loving kindness to the Present. The Buddha realized early in his quest that nothing could be achieved by a body that was starved of food, sleep, and water. It's important that you also understand this and give the body what it needs, without the deafening clamour of the Past time-body and its calls for comfort, which will lead you astray.

The needs of the Present time-body are quite simple, and yet it's extraordinary how people get it so wrong. Just look at the number of overweight and obese people, the thousands who die from an avoidable cancer every day, the millions who suppress their illness with a powerful drug.

The Present time-body just needs pure water, organic food, plenty of rest, reasonable amounts of exercise, and air that's good to breathe. Its brain and conceptual mind need to have problems to solve in order to stay sharp.

This simple approach is sabotaged by the needs of the Past time-body, which always believes it deserves rewards – of processed foods, cigarettes, alcohol and drugs – and which keeps playing the endless tape loops through the mind that eventually create anxiety, depression and worse.

Healthy habits

As you become more conscious – as the Potential centre becomes more apparent – many bad habits will naturally fall away. You can help the process by introducing habits that are healthy for the Present time-body. You've probably incorporated some, if not many, of these into your diet and lifestyle already, but here's a quick checklist of the important ones to begin exploring from Day 10 onwards. It's possible for me to write only briefly about each of these topics.

Understand your metabolic type

Many wonder if they should become a vegetarian, and ethically they should. All animals have access to the Potential centre, which is why they display great intelligence, empathy and compassion. A failure to understand this is one of the great oversights of classic evolutionary theory. Although that's the absolute truth, your body may not yet be ready to embrace a vegetarian diet.

One way to find out is to discover your own metabolic type, as some people need to eat meat until their Potential centre has become more apparent. Metabolic typing uncovers the diet that's right for your body now, and some cancer sufferers have even seen their cancer disappear just by adapting to a diet that's appropriate for their body. To discover the type you are, go to the website www.healthexcel.com for an initial review.

Maintain a correct acid/alkaline balance

Many chronic diseases are due to an acid/alkaline imbalance, and conventional wisdom has it that a high-protein diet of meats, eggs, nuts and some grains creates acid, while fruits and vegetables are alkali forming. Although this is the reason that so many suffer from a wide range of chronic diseases with the West's high-protein diet, the process is complicated by metabolic type. Foods can either acidify or alkalinize, depending on your specific type.

Don't eliminate fats from your diet

We live in a low-fat-foods society. This is entirely based on the belief that high cholesterol is bad for us, and is the cause of chronic heart disease. However, several studies suggest that cholesterol would have to be at a far higher level than what is now considered the current 'danger' mark before it starts causing damage to the heart and arteries. Furthermore, fats are necessary; they play an essential role in maintaining a healthy body, and are one of the most vital ingredients for a functioning brain.

This is why cholesterol-lowering statin drugs are often associated with memory loss and general mental decline; they reduce cholesterol to dangerously low levels. Cholesterol is even more important as we age, when we need fats and cholesterol in order to 'feed' our brain.

Avoid processed foods

As a simple rule of thumb, don't eat anything that doesn't come directly from nature. Avoid anything that's white when it should be brown, frozen when it should be fresh, or laden with preservatives, flavourings, artificial sweeteners and other 'helpful' added chemicals, rather than natural. In short, if it's been in a processing plant, don't buy it and certainly don't eat it.

Eat and drink organic

Whenever possible, try to eat and drink organic foods and drinks. Organic food is more expensive and its shelf life shorter because it hasn't been shot full of pesticides and preservatives, but at least you know you're getting more nutrition for your money.

Drink filtered water

You need to drink plenty of water every day. It's debatable just how much, but listen carefully to your body, which will tell you when and how much you need to drink. Use a good filter to ensure that all chemicals, heavy metals, parasites and fluoride have been removed first – or buy mineral water, preferably supplied in glass bottles, as toxins leach from plastic ones.

Be careful with pharmaceuticals

Prescription drugs can be important in the early stages of any disease, as they help suppress the worst symptoms, such as pain and discomfort. However, they're a short-term remedy, and you should always be looking for the underlying cause of any disease. Drugs cure nothing; they merely help make life bearable. Nevertheless, you run the very real risk of a chemical chain reaction that causes a whole host of side effects.

Get the omega-3/6 balance right

The omega 3 and 6 balance is just as important as the acid/alkaline one. The standard Western diet causes an imbalance of these essential fatty acids. The average person's ratio is 1 to 20 in favour of omega 6, when the ideal is 1 to 1. Again, this is a reflection of the amount of processed foods we eat, as vegetable oils, salad dressings and margarines are rich in omega 6. Omega 3-rich foods include linseed, cod liver oil, and fresh, coldwater oily fish such as salmon, tuna, mackerel and herring.

Get adequate vitamin D

Scientists have only recently begun to understand the vital importance that vitamin D plays in our general health, especially our mental health. The most plentiful source is, of course, sunshine, but we've been so warned off by skin cancer scares that most of us are starved of this nutrient. It's important to get an hour's sunshine every day. Top up your vitamin D levels with nutritional supplements or foods such as milk, eggs, yoghurt and fatty fish.

Keep your home chemical free

It's hard to escape all the chemicals in household products and toiletries, but you can eliminate some of them by buying 'green' and chemical-free cleaners, air fresheners, shampoos and make-up. Even the paint on our walls and the carpets under our feet are leaching chemicals all the time. Keep your chemical load to reasonable levels. A healthy immune system can handle a level of toxins, but it shouldn't become overwhelmed.

Get seven hours of sleep

A good night's sleep is essential. Without it, some of the other exercises in this programme will seem overly difficult. It's the natural end of a day that's been well spent, with activity and proper, nutritious food. For some, sleep is elusive; if you fall into that unhappy category, here are a few things to introduce into your daily regime.

Eat lightly in the evening, and don't eat too late. Ensure your last shot of caffeine is taken no later than 2.00 p.m. Don't watch TV just before you go to bed – turn it off about an hour beforehand, and instead pick up a book to read, ideally one that's either philosophical or spiritual. Listen to some calming music, such as a quiet piece of classical music or ambient, which has a hypnotic effect.

Try to quiet the mind through meditation, although researchers have found this is most effective when you do so midway through the day, and not immediately before you go to bed. Another sleep aid is blackout curtains, which make the room completely dark.

Have a good breakfast

It's a truism that the most important meal of the day is breakfast. The best breakfast should include oatmeal, one of the healthiest starts to any day, and it's healthier still when it's topped with pure maple syrup and berries.

Exercise every day

You don't have to sweat it out at the gym, but the body does need to exercise every day. A good vigorous walk is sufficient – and that means around 100 steps per minute, for 20 minutes. That's enough to get everything exercised, and to get the heart beating a little faster. When you're on the walk, breathe in deeply and fill the lungs. If a walk is difficult because of problems such as arthritis, try swimming every day.

Don't immediately kill a fever

Medicine views a fever as a major alert and it swings into action immediately to bring it down as quickly as possible. Although an unusually high fever can be dangerous, it's a necessary process. It helps kick-start the immune system, kills off germs and viruses, and even eliminates diseases such as cancer in their early stages. If you do develop a fever, monitor it very carefully and allow it to run for several days before seeking to bring down your temperature. Make sure you drink plenty of liquids and rest in a room that's properly aired.

Breathe properly

It's an extraordinary fact that most of us don't breathe properly. We often take very shallow breaths, and some of us breathe through our mouth. We should take frequent deep breaths through our nose, filling our lungs so that they swell with health-giving oxygen, and then release the air slowly through our mouth.

Keep your gums healthy

Doctors are only now beginning to understand the importance of gums and teeth to our overall health. Many health problems, especially heart disease, are associated with poor gums and teeth. Inflamed gums that frequently bleed are very likely causing problems throughout the body. In addition, it's important to keep amalgam fillings down to a minimum and avoid root canal work wherever possible.

Health researcher and pioneering dentist Weston Price discovered a direct correlation between the health of specific teeth and the health of organs in the body. He believed that root-canal work caused bacterial leakage, which is responsible for systemic autoimmune diseases such as arthritis. You're also most likely to encounter an X-ray in the dentist's chair, and so restrict these to essential work only.

Avoid smoking, and drink in moderation

It goes without saying: if you are a smoker, stop today. Self-hypnosis programmes can help wean you off the weed. With alcohol, moderation is the key. A glass of wine every so often may do more good than harm, but it's important to have quite a few alcohol-free days every week in order to allow the body to restore itself.

Mental health

If you suffer from chronic depression – particularly if you're taking prescription medication – you need to go beyond the common-sense dietary advice already given, and become a medical detective. It's vital that you don't go it alone; work closely with a qualified health professional. No matter from what discipline, he or she must be sympathetic to the idea that chronic depression has a biochemical aspect.

Although transient and mild depression is something we all suffer from time to time, chronic depression is a problem that persists. Antidepressants and other drugs such as the antipsychotics may have their place in treating serious depression, but they don't address the underlying problem. As they're very powerful chemical agents, they come with equally powerful side effects.

Almost certainly, something in your life – in your immediate environment or your diet – is causing your depression. It could be a chronic food allergy, or even leaks from a gas cooker could be responsible. Although all the exercises in the Time-Light programme are likely to be helpful in alleviating symptoms, they won't overcome a biochemical reaction. In that case, the cause has to be eliminated, and it may take several months of detox before you're feeling well again.

If you suspect that foods may be responsible for your depression, the first foods to eliminate are wheat and dairy, which together are responsible for the majority of food allergies and intolerances. If you feel depressed or down after eating a sandwich or some other wheat-based food, it's one clue that wheat could be the problem. Today there are plenty of wheat- and gluten-free alternatives, and so you don't need to go without your daily bread. The same goes for dairy products; many milk, cheese and butter alternatives are available on the market.

The cause is just as likely to be from a chemical or toxin in your immediate environment: your gas stove, your central heating system, the toiletries you use, the air freshener, or something else in your home. Environmental toxins have a cumulative effect; the body's immune system has been likened to a water barrel that starts to overflow when too much rainwater is added. Just removing a few toxins from your environment might be enough to bring down your body's overall load, allowing your immune system to begin expelling poisons in your body.

Hypothyroidism, or underactive thyroid, is another unsuspected cause of chronic depression. Although most of us are familiar with its opposite, hyperthyroidism – when the thyroid gland is overactive – many of us suffer from an underactive gland, a problem that can be brought on by diet and stress. Once diagnosed, it's relatively easy to resolve, but don't self-medicate. Instead, seek out a sympathetic health practitioner.

The Time-Light programme is not designed as a self-help course for overcoming major stress or trauma. Several modalities, such as Emotional Freedom Technique and Thought Field Therapy, have been successful in treating chronic depression and anxiety, and you may wish to explore these as a complement to this programme.

Day 11 ▶ Writing the untrue story of you

●●●●●●●●●●●●○○○○○○○○○○○

Today we're going to start writing our untrue story, but as though someone else was the author!

As with yesterday's 'Kindness to the Animal', today's exercise is a one-off. So, draw up a new page, write 'Day 11' in the left-hand corner, and in the centre, write: 'The biography of me'. Then copy across all the lessons from the previous days that are to be repeated, leaving off 'Kindness to the Animal'.

You are created by the untrue story of you, which you then play out every day in the world. We've already seen why it's untrue, or more precisely, why the psychological extract from experiences is untrue, but now it's time to tell your story.

Your story is made up of two parts: the fact and its psychological imprint, which reverberates on to make the 'you' that presents itself in the world. It's a fact, for example, that you went to such and such school, and its psychological imprint is that one of your best friends was unkind to you or mocked you one day. It's a fact that your parents were called Bob and Brenda, and the psychological imprint was they told you that you'd never come to anything in life.

Strangely, it's the facts that fill a biography, but rarely are the feelings of the main protagonist taken into account. But, then, we tend to do the same when starting up a conversation, especially with someone we don't know. Where were you born? What do you do for a living? Do you have children? Most of these questions get a response that's a few words, if that.

How much more interesting would it be if we were to ask questions about a person's feelings, the emotional extract from an experience? Instead of asking where someone went to university, we might instead ask how he or she felt about leaving home for the first time.

So today, I want you to write your biography. Usually when we write the biography about ourselves, it's called an autobiography. But I want you to be more objective. Imagine you are a reporter or a writer, finding out about his or her subject. Be dispassionate. On one side of the page, write the facts, but on the other, remember how you felt about it. That way, you make your untrue story more defined and explicit, the first steps towards ending it.

Day 12 ▶ Changing personality patterns

●●●●●●●●●●●●○○○○○○○○○

Today we're going to look at our personality traits.

Create a four- or five-page spread for Day 12, copying across all the previous exercises with the arrow beside them, and add a new section: 'Changing Personality Patterns'.

Ever since we were children, somebody has been telling us to do things differently. We were told to sit up straight and not to slouch, to chew our food properly, not to talk with our mouths full, to wash behind our ears, to go to bed on time. We were also told we had to become a better person. We should be more patient, we should respect others, and we should be kind to the elderly and to animals. We should always be polite.

The edicts about washing and eating properly relate to the Present time-body, and these all can be achieved, provided we remember to follow them. It's possible to sit up straight or chew our food properly, if we have half a mind to do so, and we can wash behind our ears, if it's not too much bother.

But we can't so easily follow the instructions to become a more patient person, respect others and be kind to the elderly, because our ability to do these things depends on the extent of the power of the Past time-body, and that, as we now know, is unconscious – or, more precisely, its movements or energy pulses are not consciously acknowledged.

The Past time-body governs most of the social niceties – such as being patient, kind and respecting others – that make the world a tolerable place. Because the Past time-body continually repeats the same pulses whenever the opportunity in present time allows, so these pulses are expressed as behaviour patterns, which, in turn, create a 'personality'.

How many times have you heard yourself say about someone, 'Oh, he's always losing his temper' or 'He's always impatient'? Patience and temper are aspects of unconscious behaviour, the automatic defining of pulses from the Past time-body. While someone is unconscious or unaware of the Past time-body, he or she can't change any personality tic.

When you look more closely at these personality traits, you see that they're a movement of Psychological time from the Past to the Present. If you're impatient, it's because you believe you know what the future holds – one of the tricks of Psychological time. Of course, you could be suddenly overcome with impatience because a delay means you may miss a train or an appointment, but often a person is impatient because of some perceived endpoint that's little more than a mental chimera.

For people in the grip of this particular mental tape, the future always holds better things than does the present moment. Whether you're walking the dog in the park, eating a meal with friends, or watching a film, your mind will eventually wish that you were somewhere else. The Czech writer Milan Kundera called one of his books *Life is Elsewhere* – and that perfectly describes how it is for impatient people.

Life is always somewhere else and at some future time. Why? Because the Past time-body is the movement of Psychological time, and the impetus that makes us work harder for a better job or a higher degree is the same one that projects a better future place and time – towards which the unconscious person is always drawn. In reality, someone in its thrall is merely postponing his or her life for an imagined and unattainable better life.

You can witness a similar movement in people who are anxious or stressed. There are many causes of stress, but one major catalyst is the imagined future. You imagine what will happen in the exam room, in the dentist's chair, during the meeting with the boss. Because of this movement of Psychological time, you become stressed and anxious. We've all experienced this some time or another – and you probably discovered that each time you were wrong. It was not as bad as you feared or at least not how you imagined it would be.

Fear is one of the big building blocks of personality. In the Present time-body, it's a natural, even healthy response. You're right to be frightened if a mad bull is rushing towards you; that fear is translated into a chemical reaction that gives you extra speed or agility when it's most needed. However, once you're over the fence and safe, the fear from the Present time-body subsides and dissipates.

It's not the same for the Past time-body. At that level, the experience becomes a 'trapped' emotion, which will be played out repeatedly, not necessarily as a fear of raging bulls, but as some undefined fear of something in the world. It's irrational and undefined, and yet it adds to the person's general sense that the world is hostile.

As we've already seen, fear generated by the Past time-body is a playing out of Psychological time. You fear a future, even though you can't know what it holds; you fear a new experience or situation, even though you've no idea what will happen; you fear the next day, because you have some sense that the world is not a friendly place. As you see, all of these are movements through time – from a barely understood past to an imagined future, bypassing the present.

As with all our thought-forms, fears can't survive in the bright light of the conscious person. They need the demi-light of the Past time-body so that they can spread their shadows over us. However, as with all shadows, they vanish in an instant when the light is switched on.

Switching on the light

So, from Day 12, we're going to switch on the light. You may already have a feeling for your own personality patterning: you may sense that you're impatient or easily angered. If you're not sure, just ask someone close to you – they'd love to tell you!

As with all these exercises, there's no right or wrong. It's not 'wrong' that you get angry easily or that you're impatient, any more than it's wrong that a fly lands on your window. I just want you to observe the fascinating movement of Psychological time.

While you're attentive, nothing will happen, of course. Nevertheless, before long you'll fall back into unconscious routines and your old pattern of impatience will re-emerge. When it does, write it down in your notebook. Simply record the fact that you were impatient and then analyze why. What were you doing at the time and what were you thinking about? Were you thinking that you could be doing something better?

If so, why did you have that thought? Notice the movement of time and record that, too.

You may completely miss the first few instances, but try to catch yourself whenever you can, and slowly you'll become more conscious of it. As I said at the beginning of the programme, this is the most difficult thing in the world to do, so don't be hard on yourself should you fall back asleep. You have a lifetime of habitual thinking to overcome.

By practising this exercise every day, the old pattern will disappear. After a while, people will start noticing. 'You don't seem to be as impatient as you used to be,' they'll say, or 'You used to get really angry about things like that – but look at you now.'

Even your parents would be proud of you.

Day 13 Seeing the world as facts

●●●●●●●●●●●●●●○○○○○○○○

Today we're going to look at our life as a series of facts – without the emotional content.

Note that today's exercise is without the arrow. This means that I want you to do this exercise on Day 13 only – don't do it again on Day 14 or any days afterwards. So, in your four/five-page-per-day log, copy the sections across from Day 12, and then, on a new page, create a new section for this exercise.

All of us have something in our life that just doesn't work. It may have to do with money, with a relationship, with our career. For today's exercise, I want you to see that the world is made up of facts. You're in debt. The washing machine doesn't work. Your boss won't give you a pay rise. The 'world' – that thing out there – is made up of nothing but facts like these. And you can't do much with a fact: you can choose to acknowledge it or not, you can act on it or not.

However, because we're unconscious beings, we do far more with facts than simply choosing to be active or passive about them. We get stressed over them, we have anxiety attacks, we can't sleep because of them, we think about them endlessly and we fret about them. At this point, the fact ceases to be a fact, and instead becomes something over which we become desperate, feel despondent, depressed, or helpless.

In sober moments, you know that worrying about a fact doesn't alter it. Indeed, it could make it worse because you're not even thinking logically any longer – and your worries could cause a pattern that attracts more of the same. However, come the wee small hours, come the time when you fall fully into the Past time-body, the same monkey mind starts churning again, and the fact takes on greater significance and becomes something over which you stress.

Writing down your problems

So, on Day 13 I want you to use your notebook to write down all the problems you have now (that's why you've set aside a full page for this exercise). It might be that you're in debt, you're without a partner, your dog has died, or you have a dental appointment you're dreading. Whatever it may be, write it down. Then, beneath that, write down another problem in your life, and so on, down the page.

Now, next to each item, I want you to create two columns. At the top of one write: Actions. At the top of the second write: Inactions. Go down the list, one by one, and consider very carefully what actions you can take. If there's genuinely absolutely nothing you can do, tick Inactions instead.

So, if you have a dreaded dental appointment, what can you do about it? You could cancel it, but that's a judgement only you can make based on any pain you're in or how urgently you need the work done. If you accept that it's necessary dental work, you have to tick the 'Inaction' column. There's nothing you can do about it other than keep the appointment. There's nothing about the situation that you can change.

There are always times when we can do nothing. Sometimes it's not within our power to change the fact in any way. This is something that we must recognize and accept. When somebody we know dies, for example, there's nothing we can do about it. No amount of fretting or sleepless nights will change the fact. Although it's natural to grieve, we must not become dominated by our grief to such an extent that we're paralyzed by it.

Let's look at another problem. Suppose that you're in debt. Have you spoken to the person or organization to which you owe the money? If not, you can put in the 'Action' column your intention to speak with them. Be specific. Note when you intend to speak to them and date the action. Could you borrow money from a relative to pay off the debt? Have you asked? Would you? If so, that's another item for the 'Action' column. Again, choose a date when you plan to get in touch.

Could you get more money from work? Have you asked the boss for a raise? How about putting yourself forward for promotion or for extra work? Have you put yourself in the boss's shoes? Can you think of things in your organization that don't work well, that could be more efficient? If you clearly see a way of improving that situation, why don't you present the problem – and your solution – to your boss? He might be so astonished that he may well give you that raise without your even having to ask for it.

These are all things you could list in your Action column and plan to do in order to address the fact that you're in debt.

When you think through your options, it's important that you plan to act on anything that comes to mind. Set yourself a definite date when you'll do it and then somehow pluck up the courage to act. If you don't, your Past time-body is again preventing you from acting by projecting into an imagined future. Until you pick up the telephone, you don't know what the response will be, so stop living in psychological time and just do it.

The same goes for your boss. You might see him as a difficult and unapproachable person, but it could be that he's looking for enterprising employees to take greater responsibility for helping to solve his business problems. Don't let the Past time-body hinder you. Be present and find out.

Once you complete this exercise, it's important to grasp that there really is nothing more you can do about being in debt, going to the dentist, or whatever situation you've chosen to examine. You have dealt with the facts that make up your world.

What you must not now do is create an internal world of the facts, as fuelled by the Past time-body. After completing the exercise, be still, be clear and say – ideally aloud – that you should now stop worrying, that everything that can be done has been done.

As with all these exercises, you'll almost certainly fall back into the patterns of the past, and the old tapes will start their old refrain. Now you can catch yourself. When you do, remind yourself there's nothing to think or worry about. You've done everything that it's possible to do.

The exercise brings its own stillness. The Past time-body will stop the automatic and unconscious fretting of its own accord. It will cease its striving for something better 'out there' and at some time in the future. It will see the fact for what it is and, in that recognition, become still.

Day 14 Finding the Recorder

●●●●●●●●●●●●●●●●●○○○○○○○○

Today, we're going to verbalize our observations and what we've learned about ourselves.

Create a new five-page section in your notebook and copy across the areas from Day 12. Add a new section from today: 'Finding the Recorder'. Then choose someone to share your feelings with and approach them about your intention to confide in them. If you're unable to find your Recorder today, put this exercise in the book for tomorrow. If for any reason it's impossible to find a suitable person, use a recording device of some sort instead. This exercise is just for today.

So far, we've been having a private conversation with ourselves. We've been observing and writing down, analyzing and recording – but now we want to make the experience more real. As we enter the third week of the programme, it's time to share our thoughts and our observations with someone else.

For years you've been hypnotized by your internal monologue – the whole 'reality-making' discourse from the Past time-body, defined and verbalized by the brain and its concepts. Its potency has come from the fact that its movement has taken place in darkness, in a shadow land of the past.

However, over the past two weeks, you've been exposing this movement to the light. You've been quietly observing the pulses and flickers from the Past time-body, and you've been recording them without judgement. You have a diary of

233

your internal monologue, and while it's now something that's become conscious, it's still a silent one.

When we experience pulses that are defined by the conceptual brain, we see the world through a filter. We may express ourselves through that filter – we might say we don't like someone, or some situation, for example – and we're rarely challenged to explain why we think the way we do. In truth, we usually can't explain the feeling we have or understand where it comes from.

As we now know, it comes from one or more of three places: the Present time-body has feelings, usually about a situation or a person, which suggest impending danger or threat. Feelings from the Present are invariably about new situations or with people we've not met before. The Potential centre, too, sends out a pulse, and this we usually call intuition. We intuitively know that something is going to happen, as though the feeling has come from somewhere beyond space and time – which, of course, it has.

However, most of our feelings arise from the Past time-body, and these form the filter through which we interpret the world from moment to moment. These feelings from the Past time-body feed off the unconscious movement to the Present time-body, and they're empowered by our silence or tacit acceptance – and so now we want to talk about them.

Saying it out loud

For this, you need the Recorder, somebody who'll listen dispassionately, without judgement or even comment, to all the feelings you've observed and recorded. The Recorder can either be someone whom you absolutely trust or – oddly enough – a complete stranger.

The most likely Recorder is somebody close to you, such as your husband or wife, sister or brother, but this can present problems, because often when we're close to people, we have things that remain secret or private, which we'd rather they didn't know. If that's not a problem with you, go ahead and adopt him or her as your Recorder.

If there isn't someone who can be a Recorder for you, the next best thing is to record your thoughts into a voice recorder. At least you're still vocalizing your thoughts and feelings from your notebook observations.

If your Recorder is a person, his or her role couldn't be easier: they have to do nothing, absolutely nothing at all. They mustn't comment, make helpful remarks, smile, or try in any way to empathize or sympathize, raise an eyebrow, look shocked, laugh out loud, burst into tears or put an arm around you.

The Recorder isn't there as a therapist or counsellor. He or she is nothing more or less than a dispassionate pair of ears. It's the very act of verbalizing your thoughts and feelings as you've recorded them in your notebook that offers the potency for change. It's like sitting in a shadowy room and imagining it full of ghosts. However, pull the curtains back, and the room is flooded with sunlight; the shadowy ghosts evaporate.

As you talk, the curtains are pulled back. The feelings lose their power, and they're finally seen for what they are.

Day 15 Right thinking, right action, right feelings

●●●●●●●●●●●●●●●●●○○○○○○○

Today we're going to look at our actions and thoughts through the model laid out by the Buddha.

Write 'Day 15' on the top left-hand corner of a new page, bring across the sections from Day 12 – include 'Finding the Recorder' again if you haven't yet completed this task – and add a new section. Note, this is not an ongoing exercise, but instead is just for today.

Today's exercise is one of taking stock. It comes right out of Buddhism, being a variation on the Eightfold Path of right view, right intention, right speech, right action, right livelihood, right effort, right mindfulness and right concentration – although similar practices are also found in Christianity.

But what is 'right'? For the Buddha, it's about steering a middle path through life, without overly engaging in it but also not withdrawing from it. This means that the actual terrain changes for each of the paths and can be open to interpretation.

But suppose we contemplate right thinking, action and feelings from the viewpoint of the Three Selves. What is right thinking, right action and right feelings in that case?

Right thinking

None of the Three Selves actually 'thinks'; as energy centres, they send out pulses that are almost immediately translated into a thought by the brain in the Present time-body. It's important to understand how this process works and what thinking actually is before we attempt to define right thinking.

Thoughts have enormous potency as they create an increase in the frequency of the pulses, which, in turn, triggers a vicious circle of thoughts and emotions. Right thinking, therefore, is composed of thoughts that are appropriate to the situation and of value. Most thinking is irrelevant and useless – indeed, most thinking is nothing more than the pointless commentary that accompanies almost every experience – and so most thinking is not right thinking at all.

For the Present time-body, right thinking is primarily problem-solving. How do I fix this? How does that work? Thoughts that arise as pulses from the Past time-body are invariably a reiteration of an old experience, which is being chewed over repeatedly, in a vain and hopeless attempt to reach resolution.

All of this is, by definition, wrong thinking. The only right thinking from the Past time-body is that which enables the viewing of a problem in context, without fanning the flames of anger. Right thinking from the Past time-body would be an attempt to understand, forgive and provide balm to a situation.

So, in practical terms, it involves seeing the other's point of view – understanding, say, why somebody did something that has upset you. With the Potential centre, we're creators and part of a unified field. Right thinking from this centre includes such thoughts as we're not alone, that, as co-creators, we're responsible for our life, and that we're compassionate to others who are suffering because they don't yet see the unified field of which they're a part.

Right action

All action is apparent in the Present time-body, even if it doesn't always start from there. Action that originates in the Present deals with immediate concerns of sufficiency, such as whether you have enough food, proper shelter and sexual satisfaction. Similar actions, originating in the Past time-body, concern having more than we need – a drive for more: more extravagant food, a bigger home, and either sex with multiple partners or pornography. Actions from the Potential centre are expressions of a sense of unity, understanding and forgiveness. As the latter is the natural state to which all life aspires, all right action, from any of the centres, is an expression of forgiveness.

Right feelings

For the Buddha, feelings involved attraction or repulsion, or were neutral. For us, feelings, or emotions, vary according to the time-bodies; for the Present, feelings concern immediate situations, giving rise to anger, fear, or surprise. The feelings should subside and disappear once the cause has gone away. For the Past, feelings are far more complicated and arise as part of a process that repeats an old experience.

Most of us often get angry all over again about some supposed hurt that we suffered in the past. For the Potential self, feelings arise from love: a realization of the unity of all things – and from understanding.

So, for Day 15, your exercise is to reflect on right thinking, action and feelings, and to observe the process. All thinking, action and feelings will become right naturally by themselves and without any effort or conscious observation of any code or precept as you follow the 21-day programme. That's true religion.

Day 16 ▸ Responding, not reacting

●●●●●●●●●●●●●●●●●●○○○○○

Today we're going to watch for moments when we react.

A new exercise today, so write 'Day 16' in the top left-hand corner of a new page and copy across the grid from Day 12. Then add a new category – 'Responding, not reacting' – that'll be part of the ongoing grid until Day 21.

Most of us react to things in the world while we remain unconscious to the movement of time from the Past time-body. As you now know, a reaction is a blind, automatic act – often resulting from a sudden rising up of emotion. Sometimes we're aware of it only after the fact. Our reactions are invariably out of proportion to the circumstance and often embarrassing to us, especially afterwards when we 'wake up'.

Reactions happen because a situation in the present resembles something that happened in the past, about which you retain an emotional charge. In other words, the new situation is one with a familiar pattern and the power to revive some unfinished business from the past. And, of course, everything that makes up the Past time-body is unfinished business.

You undergo this process on a daily basis, quite unaware that, in a sense, the present is being possessed by the Past time-body. You as your Present self are being used and lived through by the Past of dead but incomplete experience.

By comparison, a response is a considered and sober act that's reasonable and appropriate to the circumstance. If you're able to live in the Present, you respond to situations because each experience is new and different. As conscious beings in the Present, we don't have the past imprinting itself and re-establishing a familiar pattern. Not reacting doesn't mean we shouldn't respond, as the following story from the Hindu faith demonstrates.

An Indian sage so impressed a lion with his talk of peace and non-violence that the lion decided to renounce killing. Soon, word got around, and all the beast's old adversaries started picking a fight with the lion, which refused to retaliate. Eventually, the lion had enough and staggered back, bloody and bowed, to the sage.

'What happened to you?' asked the sage.

'I've just been following your teachings of non-violence. Now look what's happened to me,' said the lion, indicating its wounds.

'Yes, you're right not to kill,' said the sage. 'But I never said anything about not roaring.'

We have to roar sometimes, but as a controlled act and not a blind lashing-out from a place of emotional hurt. So, from today, your exercise is to watch for moments of reaction. While you watch you won't react, but in time you'll fall back asleep, and the Past time-body will again take control. However, as with all the other exercises in this programme, the times that you blindly react will become fewer as you slowly wake up to the movements from the Past.

Day 17 ▸ Going out into the world

●●●●●●●●●●●●●●●●●●●○○○○

Today we're going to take our understanding into the world so that we become at one with it.

Create a new five-page log for Day 17, copying across all the sections from Day 16, and adding a new section 'Going out into the world'. This exercise is a feature in all the remaining days of the programme.

A psychiatric unit had a major staff shortage and the existing employees were seriously overworked. The doctors could not see outpatients who were chronically depressed and even suicidal in any reasonable time. The nursing staff realized that they had to stay in touch with the patients, even if they couldn't see them as often as they'd like.

They needed to know the patients were taking their drugs and were not becoming suicidal – so they sent patients a postcard. On each card was a simple message: the hospital staff was thinking of them. If they really needed help, the nurses would find time for them. If they didn't hear from the patient, they sent him or her a different postcard, about a month after the previous one had been mailed.

By coincidence, around that time the psychiatric unit was one of several dozen chosen by a group of independent researchers for a study into the efficacy of certain powerful antidepressants. After interviewing a cross-section of patients from each of the psychiatric units, the researchers concluded that those from this one particular unit were faring far better than those from any other unit.

But why? The drugs were the same. The therapy was the same – in fact, the unit that came out on top was meeting with its patients less frequently than the others were. The only real difference between this unit and the others was the postcards. And that, of course, was the one difference that mattered. That simple act of contact had made the patients feel wanted, feel that someone genuinely cared. In almost every case, the patient felt that he or she mattered.

Becoming social

Such is the power of community and belonging – and that's going to be at the heart of the next exercise in our programme. Speaking out loud to the Recorder, or into your voice recorder, was the first step in going out into the world and presenting who you are to another. Now we're moving further out to a social group.

A relationship with a social group or a community is vital for our health and sanity as we seek to make conscious the internal monologue of the Past time-body. It'll also give us a wonderful sense of belonging and help to dissipate any feeling you we have that the world is hostile and unfriendly. A sense of belonging also releases us from the private prison of the Past's patterns – just as the psychiatric-unit patients discovered.

Many of us live our lives within the confines of a nuclear family. We rarely see our neighbours because our fences are too high, we don't talk to people in our community because we have security gates, and we don't go out at night because we're frightened. The world has become a reflection of our own disconnectedness.

At this point in the programme, we're working on bringing down our internal walls and allowing the daylight in to our unconscious activities – and as we lose the divisions in ourselves, the divisions between the world and us will also disappear. With this exercise, we're going to give the process a helpful, conscious push.

The point of the exercise is to engender a feeling of belonging by joining any social group, formal or informal. It could be the local drama society, the chess club, the Parent-Teachers Association (PTA), the Rotary Club, the local jogging and athletics club, or a walking group – anything you feel comfortable being a part of.

Remember, the idea of this particular exercise is not to reinforce any sense of a world out there as separate from you, but instead to rid yourself of any hostile thoughts or beliefs you might still have that the world is in some way unfriendly or even intimidating. It's also designed to help you realize that you're not 'you' any more than they are 'they': we're all together.

Day 18 ▸ Seeing your fears away

●●●●●●●●●●●●●●●●●●●○○○

Today we're going closer to the heart of things to observe how much of the way we define ourselves is based on fear.

Copy across all the sections from yesterday, writing 'Day 18' in the top left-hand corner. Add a new section, 'Seeing your fears away', which will require two columns. Put 'Fear' as the heading for one column and 'Origin' above the second.

You are afraid. It's the most common emotion at the very centre of many of your core beliefs, and it shapes most of your actions – usually as movements away from the fear. As we saw with mirror patterns, your desire for money may be, at heart, a drive away from the fear of poverty; your desire for success may be a response to the fear of being unacknowledged; your desire for enlightenment may be spurred on by your fear of unhappiness.

Although it's one of the foundational emotions, fear is hidden from most of us. We're usually unaware that we're frightened. But, of course, fear is the perfect expression of the movement of Psychological time from the past to an imagined future. Something bad may have happened in the past, and we project that into an imagined future.

Sometimes we fear a future without having experienced anything similar in the past; some of us may have a morbid fear of being poor without having had direct experience of it, but we imagine, from an amalgam of past observations, what it must be like.

When you're frightened of something that you imagine will happen to you at some future point, you're suggesting that you can see ahead with absolute clarity, and that you can determine precisely what will befall you. You may fear going to the dentist, for example, because you can 'see' exactly what'll happen to you when you get there.

Of course, nobody really knows what the future holds – and it's very rarely anything that we imagined it would be – but no matter how many times our forecasts of events don't match the reality, we still hold a fear of much of our future.

By now, you're getting a good idea of how the process works. Your Past time-body – all your time-bodies or centres, in fact – send out pulses that are immediately defined by the brain, which, in turn, superimposes thoughts, words and feelings on them. By that process, pulses from the Past time-body create Psychological time through which you see and understand the world, including yourself. All of this is the movement of Past, or dead, emotion into a quasi-living state, which happens because you're unaware of it.

The emotions themselves are half-experienced or partially understood events from the Past, and like ghosts that continue to inhabit their former homes, these feelings are relived through you in order to complete the experience. Yet it's a hopeless endeavour. While this movement is happening, you're being denied the full and rich experience of the moment, which can happen only in the full experiencing of the timeless Present.

That's the genesis and lifecycle of every thought and every emotion, and once you've observed that for yourself, you'll understand how every emotion, including the foundation ones such as fear, develops. Again, it's important not to try to stop being afraid; when people urge you 'not to be afraid', it's a pointless request while you remain unconscious, because the emotion of fear is living through you and you're unaware of that movement. Instead, it's sufficient to observe and record – and, eventually, to talk about your secret internal world to the Recorder or into your voice recorder.

Although the basic actions of observing, recording and vocalizing are useful, we have to dig a little deeper if we're to understand fear. Very few thoughts reveal themselves as being fear-based, but instead hide their original impetus.

Seeing the fear beneath the thought

As we saw earlier, most thoughts and emotions are a reaction to fear, a moving away from it. Now that you're well into your third week of the programme, you may have developed the stillness and subtlety that help to reveal the fear beneath the thought.

Fortunately, there are only a few basic fears: a fear of loss, of failure, of being unloved or feeling worthless, or of powerlessness. Any one of those is likely to be the root of many of your thoughts through Psychological time, from the Past to the imagined future.

So, for this exercise, we need an extra column – one that identifies the *originating* fear of any current thoughts you have.

At first you may be guessing, but after you try it for a few days, you'll get better at identifying exactly the fear behind the process. I call this process – in which you not only observe and record, but also analyze – 'dynamic observing', and we'll be using it again in the next exercise. Dynamic observing requires the asking of open questions, to which you don't necessarily get – or even expect – a response. For this particular exercise, it's sufficient to keep asking: What's the root fear of this thought?

A reasonable follow-on question might then be: Do I feel it's from a fear of loss? Or of failure? The key word here is 'feel'. You can't know, and your analytical brain can't help you. However, you can feel the answer, and the more you use the technique, the more you increase your ability to do so.

All the other exercises in the programme, especially those drawing on vocalizing and community, are also working towards eliminating fear. You bring your fears into the open; you finally see them for what they truly are: phantoms that try to inhabit your living being.

Day 19 ▶ Unthreading your untrue story

●●●●●●●●●●●●●●●●●●●●●●○○

Today we're going to look at the connective thoughts and feelings that give you a sense of a substantial 'you'.

Copy across all the sections from Day 18 into a new day and add a new section: 'Unthreading your untrue story'. If you're finding it difficult to write everything into five pages, simply spread your sections across to a sixth page – but remember to put the correct day at the top of each page.

In the previous exercise we introduced a new tool – dynamic observing – and you'll need it again today as you unthread the untrue story of you. Your story is your implicit narrative about who you are and why you do what you do. It's the scaffolding around the emotions that have pulsed out from your Past time-body and been given substance by the conceptual brain.

Your story is your narrative; it tells you everything about the world and yourself that you think you know. It's not true, of course, because you're imposing concepts onto a dynamic, changing present. It derives from a half-seen experience that seeks completion in the world and in the here and now, and it's based on false premises and assumptions about yourself and the world.

You won't be able to change this narrative by imposing a different set of thoughts and ideas on top of the false ones. There's no qualitative difference in our thoughts; a 'noble' thought is no different from a 'carnal' thought.

Instead, you're going to observe and record, as you've done for more than two weeks now. However, in order to unthread your narrative, you have to use dynamic observing. As we saw yesterday, this tool uses open questions and waits in silence and stillness for a response.

Looking for thought sequences

Patience is the key to this exercise. You are the attentive angler waiting on the riverbank for a pull on your fishing line. Most thoughts you have are inconsequential mutterings that roll across your mind. These you should observe and record in the same manner that you have been doing for the past two weeks.

What you're waiting for is a thought sequence based on a supportive narrative. Although no more significant than your random thoughts, the supportive-narrative thoughts will seem to be more substantial or important. They'll have a sense of urgency, necessity, or a goal to be reached. Examples include: 'I must do this because...' or 'If I can get this done, I'll...'. Both require underlying assumptions of a world from which you are utterly separate, in which effort is needed in order to succeed, and where a cause always produces a predictable effect.

Another example referred to several times in this programme is: 'If I observe my thoughts long enough, I shall become enlightened.' Look closely at the structure of that thought, and you'll see a number of assumptions underpinning it. The first and most obvious assumptions to observe are that: a) enlightenment is a state, b) it's a state worth being in, and c) you are not in that state.

Furthermore, it includes an assumption of an effort/reward trade-off, based on the age-old belief that you get what you want only from hard work. The most fundamental assumption of all, of course, is that there's a fixed 'I' who'll benefit from this state of enlightenment.

Each of these assumptions needs to be examined, but you don't have to go through a rigorous intellectual exercise in order to do so. The watchful waiting of dynamic observing will unstitch your story. Your assumptions and your narrative about them are not explicit; they're part of a mass hypnosis that has affected all of us. None of us questions who we are, and the world we inhabit; instead, it's as if we've all agreed amongst ourselves about how it must be and how we'll live in the world.

So, questions that have a sense of necessity or urgency, or a result in mind, will lead you to your tacit assumptions. Regard them as nothing more substantial than a pyramid of smoke. Nevertheless, to continue the metaphor, smoke gets in your eyes and eventually it becomes all you're able to see.

As is usually the case, you may be unconscious when you have these thoughts – in fact, by now you probably realize that thoughts from the Past time-body happen only when you're unconscious. The important thing about unthreading your story is to exercise the muscle of awareness after the fact and quietly pull apart the thought.

Let us say, as an example, that your special thought was something like, 'I must get this finished so that I can get home.' That kind of thought requires a number of concepts and associations. There has to be a correlation between the finishing of the task and your ability to leave the office, an association between finishing and reward, a concept of 'workplace' and 'home'.

There's nothing wrong with any of these thoughts, any more than there is with any other thought pattern. The exercise requires you merely to observe them and their underlying assumptions. You don't change anything, you don't beat yourself up over the thought – that would be a different movement of thought: you merely observe without judgement or desire to change.

The point is to take you deeper and to make you more conscious, like moving up to a more advanced class at the gym; you're ready for a slightly tougher workout. That's its sole purpose. While you're conscious, while you're the attentive angler sitting expectantly on the riverbank, you won't have those thoughts – or any thoughts at all.

When you are unconscious, the Past time-body will dominate. As with the other exercises in the Time-Light programme, unthreading your story will help you strengthen the focus of the Potential centre.

Day 20 ▸ The healing begins

●●●●●●●●●●●●●●●●●●●●●●●●○

Today we're going to look at ways of healing ourselves.

Another exercise – and by now you probably do need six pages per day. Copy across all the sections from Day 19 and add the new section: 'The healing begins'.

After publishing a health journal for more than 20 years, I'm staggered by how many people suffer from some illness, many of them chronic, often life-threatening, and almost all debilitating to some degree. For many reasons, there are far too many people walking around with a health challenge that they just put up with. Even if you're physically well, you may carry around some psychological problems – trauma, depression, anxiety, or worse.

Why is there so much sickness in the world when, after millions of years of evolution, we should enjoy almost perpetual health? We now know we have Three Selves, or energy centres, and that each has to work with the others if we're to be whole and free of disease. The Present time-body has to satisfy its needs without the unconscious interference of the Past time-body, which constantly subverts its desire for good, healthy nutrition with 'reward' food and drink.

The Past time-body has to become a conscious movement. The Potential centre must be acknowledged and allowed to manifest through us and into the world.

There are two possible causes of disease: those that happen in time and space, and those that happen outside of both. I don't believe these are two distinct groupings; there's a complex interplay between the two. A disease that originates outside of time and space may be amplified within the two other dimensions.

An example of this is a person who gives up the will to live, and loses his energy for life. While we live in the Present, this phenomenon couldn't happen because we'd be simple enough to live from moment to moment. However, because of the patterning from the Past, we're complex beings and can't see the simplicity of life, and that which is in front of us. As a result, life can become too much, and we lose the will to live.

Another example of this complex of time-states is in a person who continues to smoke when he's fully aware of the enormous damage he's likely to be causing. Although a smoker is chemically addicted, an incident in time and space, the continuing motivation to smoke, is taking place beyond either.

The first causes of illness – reactions that occur entirely in time and space – are well recorded, and are the stuff of medicine and biology. For example, someone becomes ill following poisoning from pollutants, such as pesticides, is injured following an accident, or reacts to a pharmaceutical drug. Time-and-space-related illnesses that may have some crossover with causes outside of these dimensions include poor diets, poor general lifestyle, hereditary issues, and contagion.

Cancer, for example, can be a disease entirely developed in time and space, such as when it's caused by exposure to toxic chemicals. It can be a crossover illness involving some morbid influence from the Past time-body. But cancer can also be the result of a diminishing of the will to live, which occurs when pulses from the Past completely overshadow the Potential centre. This can happen for a number of reasons, but when we just don't see the point of living anymore, we're separated from the Potential, a centre that becomes opaque if we're completely in the thrall of the Past time-body.

Illness can be entirely caused by the Past time-body, resulting from such thoughts as 'I told you so,' 'Look what you've done to me,' and 'I deserve this because I'm worthless/ugly/disappointing, etc.'

Psychological problems are invariably emotional. Nevertheless, it's also important to consider the Present time-body as a possible influence, since allergies and chemical reactions play a big part in depressive and other so-called mental illness. These kinds of conditions also occur when the Potential centre is completely shut off, and we lose all sense of purpose or values.

Looking for the source of disease

So what to do? Using your notebook, write down any health or psychological challenge you have right now. It may be something obvious such as arthritis, or not so apparent, such as a deep-seated emotional issue about your worth or place in the world. It's important to be still when performing this exercise. The exercises so far described should be giving you a fair degree of practice in stillness in your day-to-day life by now.

After you've described your health challenge, I want you to be very honest as you now write down from where you think it originates. It may be relatively straightforward, at the physical, time-and-space level, in which case it derives from the Present time-body. For most of you, it'll also involve the Past time-body to a greater or lesser extent, and this too should be recorded.

If you have deep depression and are at your wit's end, or you can't see the point of living, then you've lost sight of the Potential centre, and you need to write that down, too.

If your health issue is entirely at the level of the Present time-body, the remedy is relatively simple: stop or get away from that which is causing it. Many health problems are caused by a poor diet and consumption of processed 'white' foods, so look to clean up your act. If it's a crossover problem, you need to examine both your lifestyle and your Past time-body – work that's ongoing in this programme.

If your health problem is a crossover it's made up of more than one time-body; if it's entirely emotional, emanating from the Past time-body, the earlier exercises on forgiveness and gratitude are especially helpful. Forgive with your heart anyone who has hurt you and whose hurt you continue to bear; be grateful for the life you have – indeed that you are alive at all.

If you've truly lost sight of the Potential centre, forgiveness and gratitude are also important exercises, as are affirmations. These are positive statements about yourself and the world: 'The world is a friendly place,' for example, or 'I deserve all the good things that the world has for me.' You need to change your tapes consciously, and quickly. This also has the effect of stilling the Past time-body, which will allow the Potential centre to rise naturally.

From stillness comes great joy, the beginning of a healing that will last a lifetime.

Day 21 ▸ Service: The new imitation

● ●

Today we're going to do something that is in service to another.

So we come to the final lesson on the last day: service. Service to others, in subtle and explicit ways, is selflessness in action. It says that others come before me, because I'm nothing but an expression of the unified field, as they are, too. Copy across all the sections from Day 20, and add a new page, with the word 'Service' at the top.

Service lies at the heart of the spiritual life (and by 'spiritual', I mean the extent to which the Potential centre is allowed to express itself). The Potential centre is the field of unity and ultimately your true state of being, to which you'll eventually return.

The point of life is really to see that you are that and to discover to what extent you can express the Potential centre in the Present centre of time and space. How much unity, or love, can you bring into the world of seeming separation?

As we've seen throughout this book, the sense of a separate self grows as we become more time-heavy. It's demonstrated in a wide spectrum of ways: a sense of hatred of the world, cynicism, spite, anger, disappointment, depression, weariness, conceit, or, in my case, a sense of pride. All of these patterns separate you from the feeling of unity and your true inheritance. The miracle of realizing that you're infinite and eternal while living in time and space is denied you.

Service that's carried out consciously is a bridge between the sense of a separate self and the Potential centre. It can be the smallest act – such as letting someone go before you in a queue – or something so large and magnificent that it becomes the stuff of headline news, such as feeding starving children.

What you actually do in service is secondary to the act itself, because the small and the grand action are saying the same thing: I'm not separate, but an expression of a unified field.

If you're proud or conceited, as I was, it's very hard initially to respond to any experience without seeing yourself first. A proud or conceited person always thinks, 'How does this affect me?' before any other thought. For me, this sense of pride was a mirror pattern that increased in energy over the years from the initial experiences of an abusive father who consistently told me that I was inadequate and second best.

Try simple acts of kindness

So, from Day 21, I want you to do something that's in service to others. It may start small – try opening the door for someone – and the expression can grow as you volunteer to work in a soup kitchen or help feed the destitute in your neighbourhood. Whatever the act, say this to yourself as you do it: 'I do this in service to you, a fellow expression of the unified field.'

In the 15th century, the German theologian Thomas À Kempis wrote *The Imitation of Christ*, a classic work of Christian literature. In it, he outlines how, by imitating the selfless acts of Christ, we can attain Christhood (or enlightenment) in this life. The Gospels represent one of the finest expressions of selflessness and love. As love is the continual sense of unity, so its expression is the selfless act. Day 21 is, therefore, the New Imitation.

You may be wondering how it could be that, in a 21-day programme, we should be starting a new lesson today. Surely, such an important act as service should not be relegated to merely one day?

Of course not, and that's because the Time-Light programme is a continual loop that you repeat until you 'get it'. Thereafter, you don't need it anymore. Just as the child learns to write in a straight line by following the lines on a piece of paper, so you'll grow beyond the programme and the model of the Three Selves, and into the continual now of eternity and selfhood.

Afterword

Most therapies try to deal head-on with a problem from the past. Not only is this impossible, it's also unnecessary. Instead, the Time-Light programme deals with the energetic processes, and the process is the same for each experience that has been partially understood or witnessed.

Many of you may be wondering why, throughout the entire programme, I've not once spoken about meditation or, come to that, God. In fact, I've been writing about nothing else. All of the exercises achieve the aim of meditation – of stilling 'the mind', or, more precisely, the Past time-body. As that becomes more still, so the Potential self, the centre that allows you to fall back in love with your life, can rise.

Enlightenment, fulfilment, a love of life – none of these is achieved by gaining things, but by letting things go. The main thing you have to let go of is the Past time-body, the unconscious shadow that blocks out the Potential centre. While you're living in the Past and through time, you can't be present, and the Potential is apparent only in the now.

There's certainly nothing wrong with meditating, but some people do it for a purpose; they think that by being still they'll be rewarded by becoming blissfully happy or enlightened. All of this is an attempt to move from unhappiness and to an imagined state of non-unhappiness. It's part of the same process that gets the banker up every morning: If I do this, I'll get that.

Instead, my approach is meditation by stealth. I offer no reward or prize when you carry out the simple exercises of observing, recording and vocalizing. There can be no reward because 'you' are the prize you seek, but one of your time-bodies dominates and masks that truth. Any movement away from 'you' takes you further from the prize, which is you.

So, instead of encouraging movement – do this to get that – I encourage stillness, a natural consequence of observing and recording. When the Past time-body is observed, when 'you' are present, its unconscious behaviour patterns are frozen. 'You' have to become unconscious, or lose conscious awareness of the Past time-body, in order for it to function. And when it does, the whole mirage of personal narrative, the pyramid of smoke, the past living through time – all of this begins to rise up, creating your world and a 'you' in it.

The aim of this programme is to unthread the untrue story of you. Your untrue story has you going out into the world in search of happiness and in search of a self that you believe is lost. Past trauma, unhappiness and disappointment have caused a disconnection within yourself so that the Three Selves have operated independently, utterly unaware of the others.

A love of life is found only by living in the here and now. Most of us live in and through time, and in so doing, we fail to meet the challenge of the vibrant and ever-changing now. The only way you connect with the now is by living in the now, and not by being burdened by the Past, forever interpreting the now through the filters of yesterday.

The key is that there's no 'how' to get to the present; any formula consists of the Past, a dead format. While carrying out the 21-day programme, you may have noticed that while you're observing, there's nothing to record – because there are no thoughts rising up from the Past time-body.

There's much talk and speculation about the nature of enlightenment and love. In fact, they're the same thing. Love is a complete knowing that everything is unified, which is the true state of the Potential centre.

It's also knowing that there's no separate and substantial 'I' that exists independently of the world. Religions have all sorts of different words for love; the Indian religions call it nirvana, and the Christians call it heaven. Its opposite is not hate, but the sense of a lack of love. Hell is the sense of disunity and separateness. There's nothing more hellish than feeling utterly alone, helpless and separate.

If we're unconscious, we're living to some degree in hell. The poor souls who are suicidal are at the far edge of a sense of extreme separation and can see no way out of their despair of utter aloneness. The urge to commit suicide is also an indication of the extent of your blindness to the Potential centre in you. A realized or enlightened person knows that he is the Potential, that there's no division in life, and that we're all one. Truly knowing this is a coming home, a return to Eden, the end of your untrue story.

Your path has taken you to this book and to this point, and there's no going back. Now the path disappears; it has no beginning or end, no destination, no reward. It's a continual loop of awareness. And so, with pencil in hand, I invite you to start with me again from Day 1 and into eternity.

Glossary

In creating the philosophy of the Three Selves and the Time-Light programme, I've invented some new terms or used existing terms in slightly different ways. Here's a glossary of these terms for ready reference.

Addictive behaviour patterns: Most of us have addictions, whether to drink, food, sex or shopping. These are repetitive behaviours based on experiences. They arise from the Past time-body, specifically the Psychological self, and they're an attempt to rekindle a past sense of oneness or completeness, but result from a wrong association.

If, for example, you had a sense of completeness while holding a glass of wine, you might wrongly identify that sense with alcohol, and so seek to experience it again through drink. Ironically, any strengthening of the Past time-body through addictive behaviour reduces those moments of unity which arise from the Potential centre.

Ultimately, any movement from the Past time-body seeks completion through understanding. Seen that way, an addiction is a pattern that seeks completion and an end. It comes from ecstasy, joy and a sense of unity – not from sadness. Some addictions do have a biochemical component, and it's important to tackle these within the Present time-body.

Associated addictions: Most of the addictions I discuss are associated addictions. They come about when an oceanic feeling of love or unity occurs while you are doing something else. That something else, such as driving a sports car, becomes the object or action associated with the feeling, and so you seek to repeat it. (See also Psychological Witchcraft, p.270.)

Changing the tape: A technique in which you consciously change thought patterns. Most of us have a pattern in our life – a difficulty holding down a job, say, or saving money – based on a pattern of thought, of which we're unaware, that helps to create our reality. These thoughts, in turn, are based on a series of assumptions, which, when examined, are arrived at from surprisingly little information, often just a few experiences. All these patterns begin as a pulse from the Psychological past.

Clear experiences: A clear experience is one that leaves no energetic footprint; it's a full experience in the moment. Very few of us have clear experiences. Most of us have partial experiences, usually based on our own limited point of view and seen through the eyes of our own Past time-body. A partial experience leaves an energetic print in the Past time-body and will continue to rise up through the Present time-body in order to complete the experience.

Commander self: The commander self is one of the greatest fictions that affect humanity. It's the sense that there's a 'real' you, which is consistent and enduring, that controls all thoughts and emotions. The belief in a commander self is at the heart of many therapies, which suggests that 'you' – a commander self – suppress unpleasant thoughts and place them into a subconscious, and that this same 'you' can discover these thoughts and work on them.

Direct addiction: Unlike an associated addiction, a direct addiction is one in which someone takes a drug, such as LSD, specifically to create an oceanic feeling. For this form of addiction to end, the addict needs to experience the feeling of love and unity naturally.

Displaced concept: An impulse from the Past time-body seeks final understanding and resolution of an experience that was not completely understood. It does so only through the Present time-body within time and space. However, this is a futile endeavour as the original situation and characters have changed or have died. The best the conceptual brain can do is to create either a pattern, so that the experience is repeated as closely as possible to the original situation, or a displaced concept, where a sense of loss may be transferred to a different person or situation.

Dynamic observing: Most of us sleepwalk through our lives. We're barely conscious of our own thoughts or the world around us. Dynamic observing is a way of being sensitive to every influence and seeing yourself in the experience, too. It also involves asking yourself open questions, and feeling the responses, rather than intellectualizing them. Often, the closest we get to a dynamic observation is when we're suddenly embarrassed. At that moment, we clearly see others and ourselves.

Emotions: It's natural to have emotions. All Three Selves trigger emotions – the Present self has immediate emotions related to the world in time and space, such as fear, anger, kindness, grief and generosity, while the highest emotion of the Past self is empathy. The Past self is also the store of past emotions related to previous experiences, and these are replayed in the Present. Only the Potential centre expresses true love, a sense of unity with all things.

ESTs (Events outside Space and Time): Although we appear to live in a world of time and space, governed by natural laws, we all occasionally have experiences that seem to contradict these physical laws. We experience this at a mundane level whenever we get a phone call from someone we've been thinking about or become aware of people staring at us while our back is turned. Countless instances of telepathy, clairvoyance, near-death experiences and premonitions have been recorded, and a good number scientifically verified. I call these experiences Events outside Space and Time (ESTs).

Facts: The world is made up of facts. It's a fact that there's a war, it's a fact that I'm in debt, it's a fact that my car has broken down. We give these facts meaning by investing them with values and emotions. We accentuate facts and often make any situation worse by becoming emotional about them. This also prevents us from acting coherently to improve the existing situation. As the world is made up only of facts, we can do just two things in the world: act, if it's within our power to do so, or do nothing.

Forgiveness: Forgiveness is for your own benefit, not for the person you're forgiving. It's a letting go of a past energetic imprint.

Letting go and forgiveness are the natural consequences of fully understanding a situation. Only when you fully understand an experience by using dynamic observing will you naturally forgive and so let go. Dynamic observing occurs at a point of great stillness, when all three time-bodies are coordinated. You're then fully conscious.

Fully witnessed: A fully witnessed experience takes account of the complete situation, its origins, and the characters involved, including their motivation. In that instance, a situation is fully understood, and is complete. As such, it doesn't seek reiteration in the Present time-body in order to find complete understanding and resolution. An experience that's fully witnessed leaves no energetic trace in the Past time-body.

Genius: The prevailing view is that genius is a quality of the brain, and is the next logical step on from being extremely intelligent. This isn't always the case: a genius from the world of the arts, for example, may have an average intelligence. According to the Three Selves model, genius is the degree to which someone is sensitive to his or her Potential centre.

Most moments of special inspiration happen in a way that the person can't account for. An insight seems to happen 'out of the blue'; in fact, it occurs outside of space and time, and enters the world through the recipient's brain. The brain is therefore merely the receiver of inspirational pulses from the Potential centre, and a genius has a brain that's 'tuned in' at an appropriate moment.

Hannah filter: Hannah was the name of Sir Isaac Newton's mother. It's a palindrome – it reads the same backwards and forwards. Newton proved that white light is made up of a spectrum of colours, from the one to the many. I've used this as a metaphor for the Three Selves that arise from the Potential centre, the field of being. Ultimately, the three return to the one (just as, in reverse, a spectrum of colours can be turned into white light).

Hungry mind: This occurs when the Present combines with the Psychological past to create an energy pattern that suggests the next new thing – be it a car, a book or a house – will make you forever happy, or provide the missing key. It can also be an element of addictive behaviour.

Knowledge past: This is an important self from the Past, where skills and expertise, such as fixing a broken object or changing a tyre, live. It's the self that allows us to operate in the world.

Mega-feelings: The Past time-body is made up of partially understood experiences that pulse into the Present time-body, where they become a thought or feeling through the conceptual mind. We rarely define or challenge these feelings, but instead assume that they somehow inform us about reality and the world. Mega-feelings are the collective feelings that feed our unquestioned assumptions, such as that 'I' am somehow permanent and substantial, and that there's a world out there which is separate from my body.

Mirror patterns: Either you repeat the patterns from your past or you react against them – in which case they become mirror patterns. In either case, you're acting unconsciously from the past. A mirror pattern is the exact opposite of your own experience, such as when a woman who was not allowed to go to ballet classes as a child pushes her own daughter into attending.

Narrative past: This layer of the Past time-body is the story of 'you', and it defines who you are in the world. On its own, the Narrative past is innocuous, but when fused with the Psychological past it can become volatile. This combination of past selves lies at the root of most wars and strife, which are fuelled by a sense of difference, whether in nationality, creed or religion, and by a sense of injustice or wrong from the Psychological past.

Nostos: A Greek word for coming home. Nostos is the ultimate aim of life, but it's achieved only by the conscious person – someone who fully understands with no trace of a Psychological past in the Past time-body (the Narrative and Knowledge past selves survive this process). Home is the Potential centre arising naturally in the Present time-body, and the gate that bars entry is the Psychological self.

Nostos, or homecoming, occurs when this Psychological self comes to know itself. This process has been illustrated in different cultures and religions throughout the ages, from the biblical banishment from the Garden of Eden to the homecoming of Odysseus in Homer's *Odyssey*.

Past time-body: One of the Three Selves, the Past time-body is the accumulation of all experience. It comprises three sub-selves: the Narrative, the Knowledge and the Psychological selves. It sits between the Present and Potential selves, and although it exists outside of space and time, it invariably identifies with the Present as it seeks to relive partially observed experiences.

However, it's also aware of the infinity of the Potential. This creates a tension, a yearning in the Present that's never satisfied. The highest expression of the Past time-body is empathy.

Potential centre: One of the Three Selves, the Potential is the ground of being and the field of all possibility. Although the primary source for life, it sits outside of space and time. The Potential is a unified field that seeks to know itself through the relative reality of separation and the multiplicity of life.

Depending on the culture, it's also known as consciousness, Atman, God, Mind, the Christ, Krishna or Brahma, nirvana, the Buddha and the Father. In its passive state, it's the observer behind sight, and provides the sense of a continuous self that exists in all states, waking or sleeping.

Present time-body: The one self that exists in its own creation of influences from the world. Because the Present is the only self that's palpable, it becomes diseased from direct causes in the environment and from emotions trapped in the Past self.

Psychological past: One of the three sub-selves in the Past time-body, this is the centre for all experience that's not fully comprehended or observed. As all of life is a movement towards greater understanding, so the Psychological past seeks to re-enact these experiences through the Present time-body in order to reach completion with full understanding. It's the one barrier between you and enlightenment, but a necessary one as it enables you to become conscious.

Psychological Witchcraft: This occurs as the result of an ecstatic moment. As we wish to repeat and understand it, we attempt to recreate the same situation in which we had the original experience in order to invite back the feeling that occurred at the time. This is a form of witchcraft and the root of addictive behaviour.

Pulses: The Three Selves are energy patterns; as such, they communicate by means of pulses or waves, which are immediately interpreted by the brain in the Present time-body as thoughts, emotions and concepts. An energetic pulse precedes every thought and emotion.

Reacting: Most of us react to a challenge in the Present. This invariably involves a blind or involuntary lashing-out because it's a pattern we already recognize. If an experience is completely new – which becomes increasingly unlikely as we age – we don't have a referencing pattern and so instead simply respond.

The Recorder: We live internal lives. Our thoughts become like giants to us and take on enormous significance. The Recorder can be either another person or a voice recorder, to whom (or which) we talk about our thoughts, especially as we've recorded them in our notebook. The Recorder is no more or less than a set of ears, who listens without comment, reassurance, understanding, or any communication other than the acknowledgment that he or she has heard you.

Responding: This is the appropriate way to meet any experience and challenge. It's measured and conscious and, as such, defuses a tense or angry situation. To respond requires us to see the situation as utterly new and unique, for which we have no preceding pattern. In theory, every experience in the

Present is new – by definition that must be so – but usually we react because it's a pattern we recognize from a past and incomplete experience.

The therapy triangle: At the heart of almost every therapy is the unspoken assumption that there's an 'I' with a problem that needs resolving. This creates the typical therapy triangle of the person with the problem, the problem itself and the therapist.

This would suggest that this 'I' is somehow independent of the problem, and will be happier or a better person once we're less angry, or have more confidence, and the like. However, we fail to see that there's no difference whatsoever between the sense of a person and the problem itself; in fact, the person is created by the problem.

The thought thinks the thinker; the emotion creates the feeler. The desire to be better is from the very same energy source that's causing the anger or sense of worthlessness. Acknowledging the problem in this way may achieve some improvement, but ultimately it will perpetuate it. True healing is achieved when the whole process of thought and emotion – that which creates the thinker and feeler – is seen very clearly. In that clarity, it dissolves.

Thought locating: All thoughts begin as a pulse from one of the Three Selves. As you become more sensitive, you'll be able to recognize the source of each of the pulses.

Three Selves: For 3,000 years, philosophers and now scientists and neurosurgeons have tried to arrive at a definition of the self and consciousness. Today, the primary theory holds that the sense of self is nothing more than neural firings in the brain between the left and right hemispheres and so a fiction created from the body. However, this interpretation fails to capture the true richness and complexity of the human experience.

I believe the sense of 'I' is the sum total of pulses from the Three Selves, energetic patterns that I call the Present, the Past (itself made up of three sub-selves), and the Potential, or ground of being. The sense of self is dependent on the dominant pulse at any one time, which is why 'you' constantly change; the only constancy is in the Potential centre, and that's impersonal.

Time: Two of the Three Selves produce variations of time. The Present creates and imprints serial time – as we understand the concept of time, something relentlessly moving forwards – onto the eternal. The Psychological past creates Psychological time. All of thought is a movement of Psychological time, from the past to some future, be it moments ahead.

Time-heavy: As we age, we become time-heavy with the burden of experience that still sits as an energetic print in the Psychological past. And as we become more time-heavy through the unconscious pulses from the Psychological past we become unhappier and less able to feel any sense of joy.

Time-light: Most children are time-light because they've not accumulated experiences that they've not fully understood. When we're time-light, the dominant pulses emanate from the Present time-body and the Potential centre, from where the sense of joy and unity derives. We feel a sense of pleasure from experiences in the Present time-body, but unless these experiences are clear, they'll imprint into the Psychological past and create a pattern of pulses that seek repetition.

Universal subjectivity: We all believe we're having separate and individual experiences, even though we are, in fact, expressions of the same unified field. I call this phenomenon 'universal subjectivity' – everyone thinks he or she is separate and having a separate experience within a body, and yet no one actually is.

References

Chapter 3

1. *Psychological Bulletin*, 2007; 133: 1007-37
2. *Personality and Social Psychological Review*, 2008; 12: 370-89
3. *European Heart Journal*, 2010; 31: 1065-70
4. *Clinical Cancer Research*, 2010; 16: 3270-8
5. *European Journal of Human Genetics*, 2007; 15: 784-70
6. Yehuda, R. *Treating Trauma Survivors with PTSD* (American Psychiatric Publishing Inc., 2002)

Chapter 4

1. *American Journal of Preventive Medicine*, 2009; 37: 389-96
2. *Journal of the National Cancer Institute*, 2010; 102: 991-2
3. *Archives of Pediatrics & Adolescent Medicine*, 2009; 163: 1135-43
4. *Arthritis Care & Research*, 2009; 61: 1554-62

Chapter 5

1. *Nature Neuroscience*, 2009; 12: 1222-3
2. *The Canadian Medical Association Journal*, 1965; 92: 647-51
3. Radin, D. *The Conscious Universe* (HarperEdge, New York, 1997)
4. *Daily Nation*, March 2001

5. Eason, C. *Psychic Power of Children* (W. Foulsham & Co, Slough, 2005)

6. Dossey, L. *The Power of Premonitions* (Dutton, New York, 2009)

7. ibid.

8. Currie, I. *You Cannot Die* (Somerville House, 1978)

9. Schmicker, M. *Best Evidence* (Writer's Club Press, Lincoln, 2000).

Chapter 7

1. *Proceedings of the National Academy of Sciences*, 2010; doi: 10.1073/pnas.1009112107.

Acknowledgements

A book purports to have one author; in fact, many make a book possible. From Hay House Publishers, I thank Michelle Pilley for seeing the worth in the book and for making it a better one.

I thank my two children, Caitlin and Anya, for their help and encouragement, even though they didn't know they were proffering it. I acknowledge my life-long debt to my wife and soul-mate, Lynne McTaggart, who has helped me on every stage of this process, both on and off the page.

ABOUT THE AUTHOR

Carl Studna

Bryan Hubbard has an extensive and versatile background as a journalist, editor, publisher and author, and is owner and managing director of two publishing companies, and publisher and co-editor of the international magazine *What Doctors Don't Tell You*, now published in nine countries.

Bryan holds a BA in philosophy from London University and a degree-level qualification in journalism from Harlow College. After winning first prize in a national writing award, he began his career on local newspapers and became one of the country's youngest news editors, securing the position at the age of 18.

Prior to launching his own publishing group, Bryan held editorships of a variety of prominent EMAP and Financial Times Group titles, including *Money Week, Money Business* and *Small Company Investor*. He also worked for the Confederation of British Industry, converting their annual programme into a highly popular book. He has edited and written about conventional and alternative medicine for 26 years. He and his wife, author Lynne McTaggart, live and work in London with their two daughters.

www.bryanhubbard.net